BRAZIL

BRAZIL

AN INTERIM ASSESSMENT

by

J. A. CAMACHO

SECOND EDITION

GREENWOOD PRESS, PUBLISHERS
WESTPORT, CONNECTICUT

The Library of Congress has catalogued this publication as follows:

```
Library of Congress Cataloging in Publication Data

Camacho, Jorge Abel, 1908-
     Brazil; an interim assessment.

     Reprint of the 1952 ed.
     Bibliography:  p.
     1.  Brazil.
[F2508.C18   1972]          918.1          78-138144
ISBN 0-8371-5601-7
```

The Royal Institute of International Affairs is an unofficial body which promotes the scientific study of international questions and does not express opinions of its own. The opinions expressed in this publication are the responsibility of the author.

Originally published in 1952
by Royal Institute of International Affairs, London

Reprinted with the permission
of Oxford University Press

Reprinted from an original copy in the collections
of the University of Illinois Library

First Greenwood Reprinting 1972

Library of Congress Catalogue Card Number 78-138144

ISBN 0-8371-5601-7

Printed in the United States of America

CONTENTS

	page
Preface	vii
Preface to Second Edition	viii
Introduction	1

I. Contrast: Geographic, Economic, and Demographic
Main Geographical Features	5
Climate and Rainfall	7
Geographical Zones	9
Mineral Wealth	10
Population	12
Living Standards	14
Racial Origins	17
Occupations of Population	19

II. Experiment: Racial, Economic, and Political
Causes of Miscegenation	22
Racial Elements and Immigration	24
Early Economic Development	27
Economic Cycles	29
Early Political History to 1822	35
Political History: the Empire (1822–89)	39

III. Emancipation: Political, Economic, and Cultural
Political History: the Republic (1889–1932)	42
Industrial Development	47
Transport	51
Foreign Investments	53
Cultural Development	55
Literature	57
Music	59
Architecture, Sculpture, and Painting	60
Science, Technology, and Medicine	61

IV. Example: Colonization and Foreign Policy
Self-colonization	63
The Work of General Rondon	65

Contents

	page
Forty-seven Years of Peace	68
Brazil and the First World War	72
Relations with the United States	73
Brazil and the Second World War	75

V. THE SCENE TODAY: POLITICAL, ECONOMIC, AND SOCIAL

The First Vargas Regime	79
The 1945 Elections	85
Political Developments from 1945 to the 1950 Elections	86
Religion	90
The Dutra Administration	91
Economic Position Today	93
Hydro-electric Power	100
Steel	101
Staple Foods	101
Coffee	103
Cotton	104
Fruit and Cacao	104
Rubber	105
Other Vegetable Products	105
Terms of Trade	105
Banking System	106
Education	107
Press	108
Radio	110
Constitution	111

VI. THE FUTURE	115
BIBLIOGRAPHY	119
INDEX	121

MAPS

1. Principal Rivers and Mountains	8
2. The Principal Zones	9
3. Principal Cities	14
4. The States and Territories	15

PREFACE

I MADE numerous visits to Brazil before the war; my last visit was in 1946. I never thought then of writing a study of the country; if I had I would have made better use of my time. As it is, I have had to rely on memory, existing works, Brazilian newspapers, official reports and statistics, and, above all, on the assistance of friends. I am particularly indebted to *Brazil*, edited by Lawrence F. Hill, from which the contributions on science (by Francisco Venancio Filho), art (by Mario de Andrade), music (by Luiz Heitor Corrêa de Azevedo), and literature (by Samuel Putnam) were invaluable for the necessarily abbreviated passages on these aspects of Brazilian cultural development; similarly, Mr J. Fred Rippy's *Historical Evolution of Hispanic America* was the basis of the section dealing with the various presidential administrations from the fall of the Empire until 1932. The statistics quoted are nearly all taken from one or other of the statistical annuals of the Brazilian Institute of Geography and Statistics or from similar publications of the Brazilian Ministry of Foreign Affairs. The most recent available figures are everywhere given, but unfortunately only an advance synopsis of the 1950 census has been published so far.

Among the friends who have helped me I would wish to thank particularly H.E. the Brazilian Minister-Counsellor at the Brazilian Embassy in London, Senhor Jayme Sloan Chermont, who read the final draft and made helpful corrections and additions; Mr W. A. Tate, Brazilian Programme Organizer of the B.B.C., who lent me books and statistics and gave me information obtained during his many years' residence in Brazil; Mr Alan Murray, until recently correspondent of *The Times* in Rio de Janeiro; Senhor João Ribeiro Penna, secretary of the Folha group of newspapers in São Paulo; Senhor Antonio Callado, of Rio de Janeiro; Mr John Brittan, until recently B.B.C. representative in Rio de Janeiro, and Mr Edward Skelton, the present B.B.C. representative; Mr Cecil Haven; and by no means least the various members of the Chatham House Committee, many of whose useful comments have been incorporated in the text. But I should make

Preface

clear that the opinions expressed in this study are entirely my own, except where otherwise stated.

Brazil is developing and changing very quickly; no study or assessment of the country can be definitive; least of all a brief study such as this one. That is why I have called it an interim assessment.

J. A. C.

October 1951.

PREFACE TO SECOND EDITION

For the second edition of this study I have been able to include many statistics for the year 1951 and have quoted these in the place of the 1948 figures appearing in the first edition. Not all the analyses of the 1950 census have yet been completed, which explains why in some cases the only available statistics are those of the 1940 census. I am indebted to many friends for useful and constructive comments; I would add to those mentioned above, Mr P. R. Haydon, Australian Minister to Brazil from 1950 to 1953, Mr J. S. Carolin, Mr H. A. Holley, and Mr D. Blelboch.

I would also add that the speed of the development of Brazil has not abated and that this study can do no more than suggest the future importance of the country.

J. A. C.

January 1954.

INTRODUCTION

THE study of a nation of some fifty-five million people, inhabiting the fourth largest political area in the world and the second largest in the Western Hemisphere, needs no justification. The problem is what sort of study to make, and to what extent it can add to the general understanding of Brazil. Traditionally, it should be assembled under a few main headings dealing in turn with the geography, the people, the history, the economy, and so on; the result, assuming accuracy, would be a useful book of reference. Alternatively, there is the impressionist approach; the traveller's tales filled with colour and as often as not most readable when least accurate. The problem is to combine the facts of the first with something of the interpretative value of the second.

There is always the danger in the study of a country not one's own that the differences, however unimportant, will loom larger than the similarities, however fundamental. In the case of Brazil the danger is there but it matters less; for Brazil and Britain are as different from each other as it is possible for two nations belonging to the same civilization and culture to be, though this does not mean that the two nations have not many points of contact. The fact is that Brazil belongs essentially to the West European cultural group—what we might now call the Atlantic civilization. Beyond this, Brazil is a country that presents many unique features: violent contrasts, new types of development, a possible pattern for the development of the underdeveloped areas of the world, an example to other nations in a similar stage of development in the conduct of foreign affairs and new experiments in self-colonization. Brazil, in fact, is a fruitful field for study as the first tropical colonial area ever to give signs of wholly achieving its emancipation.

Politically, Brazil became an independent empire under Dom Pedro I in 1822; but nominal political independence is not necessarily emancipation. It was Disraeli who said: 'Colonies do not cease to be colonial because they are independent.' The nations of Latin America did not lose their colonial characteristics overnight because the power of Spain in the New World was finally broken at the battle of Ayacucho in 1824. Their political

Introduction

independence they mostly gained in the early nineteenth century; their cultural emancipation they have been achieving ever since; their economic freedom they are only now beginning to attain. The political development of Brazil differs from that of the other countries of Latin America in that independence was achieved peacefully, and that for a long period there was uninterrupted constitutional monarchical rule; modern developments have reflected the political *malaise* of the world, as well as Brazil's growing relative importance as a world power and as one of the leading nations of Latin America.

Cultural emancipation is not a subject that can be given adequate treatment in a study of this nature. Brazil belongs to Western culture, but it has not passively accepted the benefits; on the contrary, it has made positive contributions. Brazilian architects and painters, musicians and scientists, doctors and inventors, have made, and continue to make, a significant contribution. In letters, the great names are less well known, perhaps because Portuguese is so little studied. In aviation, in modern tropical architecture, in the development of anti-venom serums, in mass radiography, and the study of tropical diseases, Brazilians are in the vanguard. Certainly it is a long time since Brazil could be fairly described as culturally colonial.

The rise in the standard of living, however unevenly achieved, the development of industry, the change from the colonial one-product economy to a broader-based and independent, if by no means self-sufficient, economy, are significant changes. What happens in Brazil today does not go unnoticed in the other tropical countries of Latin America; it may have some influence on the political leaders of the newly independent nations of the East; and it undoubtedly has some bearing on the future of tropical Africa. In all these fields Brazil constitutes an experiment that repays study.

It is perhaps in the field of racial relations, however, that the Brazilian experiment has most to offer. It would be rash to try to make an exact analysis of the ethnographic make-up of the Brazilian people, but it is safe to say that of all the major independent countries of the world, Brazil has a larger proportion of negroes than any except South Africa; and yet in Brazil the negro question is not a problem. The process of complete miscegenation is not yet ended, and may last for generations, but it is clear already that in Brazil it is unlikely that there should ever be a

Introduction

colour problem. The future that haunts South African Nationalists, the alarming problem that confronts the United States, the peril of Communist exploitation of racial antagonisms—all these Brazil has avoided. As long ago as 1912, James Bryce could write[1] that the Portuguese Brazilians do not feel towards the negro race 'that repression which marks the attitude of the whites to the negroes in North America and South Africa'.

The Brazilian lower class [he continues] intermarries freely with the black people; the Brazilian middle class intermarries with mulattoes and quadroons. Brazil is the one country in the world, besides the Portuguese colonies on the East and West coasts of Africa, in which a fusion of the European and African races is proceeding unchecked by law or custom. The doctrines of human equality and human solidarity have here their perfect work. The result is so far satisfactory that there is little or no class friction.

Bryce perhaps overstates the case. It would be wrong to say that today there is no racial prejudice whatever; but certainly there is far less than anywhere else.

But Brazil has other achievements to its credit. Although the country is only now achieving maturity, in spite of an often unsettled political outlook, in spite of an uneven and erratic political development, in one respect it provides an example to the world. In international relations, Brazil has in the main revealed a sanity, restraint, and measure of good will hardly to be equalled by any other of the world's larger Powers. Only five times has independent Brazil been involved in war: against the tyrant Rosas of Argentina; against the Provincias de la Plata, over the fate of what is now Uruguay; against the dictator López of Paraguay; against the Germany of Wilhelm II; and against Hitler. Brazil has common frontiers with seven of the other nine republics of South America and with the three Guianas; and with most of them boundary disputes have been settled by negotiation and arbitration. Even when civil strife arises, it is less violent and causes less bloodshed than elsewhere. The Brazilian is essentially peaceful. As a nation, Brazilians look for no aggrandisement, they look for no quarrel, and they nowhere threaten the peace of the world.

Brazil provides examples in other directions. One is colonization: for Brazil is a colonial Power in a far truer sense than, for

---

[1] *South America: Observations and Impressions* (London, Macmillan, 1912), pp. 179–80.

Introduction

example, Italy ever has been. That the territories Brazil is colonizing lie within its own frontiers matters not at all; for many of them are at least as remote from the modernity of Rio de Janeiro and São Paulo as, say, Dar-es-Salaam or Entebbe from metropolitan London. Large areas of the interior of Brazil have been colonized by Europeans and Brazilians during the last hundred years, and the work of General Rondon has struck a new note: his has been the task of assimilating more territory, and its nearly uncivilized Indian inhabitants, into the national life of Brazil. In the matter of immigration, Brazil has useful experience to offer other under-peopled countries. Land of contrast and experiment, one of the most important features of Brazil is the fact that it is in process of completing not only its political, but also its cultural and economic emancipation.

CHAPTER I

CONTRAST: GEOGRAPHIC, ECONOMIC, AND DEMOGRAPHIC

MAIN GEOGRAPHICAL FEATURES

Geographically, Brazil is larger than is generally thought; Mercator's projection reduces the apparent size of tropical areas. On a globe, Brazil can be seen to be even larger than the United States (without Alaska). Its area is 8,516,037 square kilometres (3,288,383 square miles).[1] Its territory extends through the same number of degrees of latitude as Chile (29°), and a greater number of degrees of longitude than any other nation in Latin America (27°). Its widest span from east to west (2,690 miles) is approximately equal to its longest distance from north to south (2,670 miles). The whole of Brazil is to the east of the longitude of New York. From London or Antwerp the distance to Recife (4,175 miles) is not much greater than the distance to New York (3,370 miles). The distance of Brazil's great trading ports of Santos and Rio de Janeiro to New York is not very different from their distance to European ports. Brazil's great north-eastern bulge reaches into the mid-Atlantic; Recife is only 1,700 miles from West Africa. For the purposes of world trade, and from the point of view of world strategy, Brazil enjoys a highly favourable and important position.

There are no peaks in Brazil to compare with Aconcagua, Chimborazo, and Cotopaxi, although it occupies half the area of the continent in which the Andes are situated. Except for a short stretch of the Serra do Divisor, on the Peruvian frontier, the Andes do not touch Brazil, but they have a profound influence on the country; first, it is among them that rise many tributaries of the Amazon; and second, they have presented a formidable

[1] *Anuário estatístico do Brasil*, 1950 (Rio de Janeiro, Instituto Brasileiro de Geografia e Estatística).

5

Brazil

barrier and have saved Brazil from hostilities with any of its western neighbours. Important geographically are the ranges of mountains to the north, for they mark the frontier with Venezuela and the Guianas, and are the watershed between the Orinoco and its tributaries, the Essequibo and the other Guiana rivers to the north, and the Amazon tributaries to the south. The Serra de Pacaraima is the western end of these northern ranges and rises to heights of over 8,000 feet; the Tumucumanque in the east, on the frontier between Brazil and French Guiana, falls to below 3,000 feet.

There are two mountain ranges that run from the south in a north-easterly direction. They are roughly parallel. The more inland of these runs from the east of the state of São Paulo where it is known as the Serra da Mantiqueira, and eventually turns north as the Serra do Espinhaço to form the eastern rim of the São Francisco river basin. The highest peak in the Mantiqueira range is the Pico das Agulhas Negras (9,144 feet). The other range is the Serra do Mar, which crosses the north of the state of Rio Grande do Sul and then follows the coast to end in the Serra dos Orgãos behind Rio de Janeiro, reaching there a height of more than 7,000 feet. In that part of the Serra do Mar known as the Caparaó is to be found the Pico da Bandeira, the highest peak in the country (9,482 feet).

There are also mountains in the central plateau of Brazil rising in places to heights of about 4,500 feet. Between them and the Mantiqueira-Espinhaço range the São Francisco river flows northwards; the tributaries of the Paraná flow west and south, and the Paraná eventually flows into the River Plate. At the extreme west of the central plateau rises the Paraguay, flowing south and also destined ultimately to swell the waters of the River Plate. For the rest, the central plateau is drained to the north into the vast Amazon basin; and it is of course the Amazon that overshadows every other geographical feature of Brazil.

The Amazon is the third longest river in the world; it is 4,500 miles from the source of the Ucayali to the sea. Only the Nile, and the Mississipi–Missouri are longer, but the Amazon drains a far larger area, and along it flows a much greater volume of water. Six South American countries are in part drained by the Amazon, and its basin is estimated to extend over 2,300,000 square miles. It is navigable by ocean-going ships as far as Manaus,

Contrast: Geographic, Economic, and Demographic

1,042 miles from the sea. Some vessels go as far as Iquitos, 2,300 miles from the Atlantic, and river boats can navigate a further 500 miles up-stream. The Amazon is said to have over a thousand tributaries and some 30,000 miles of navigable waterways. It flows almost throughout, through dense forests; large areas have not even been explored. Rubber, hardwood, nuts, and many other riches are to be found in the Amazon basin; food can be grown, and it has been shown that man, even the European, can live there in health. But the cost of making this possible is high—as one or two full-scale experiments have proved—and in spite of the existence of some towns and villages, in spite of some exploitation of a few natural products, of which rubber is the most important, by far the greater part of this vast area is as yet producing nothing for mankind. The meagre population, outside a relatively large centre like Manaus, is a prey to such diseases as malaria and hookworm.

CLIMATE AND RAINFALL

The rivers and mountains do not provide the only contrasts of Brazil. The rainfall, too, exercises a profound influence. In general, in the more inhabited areas, the rainfall is favourable to man and his needs, both in quantity and in its distribution over the seasons of the year. In the greater part of Brazil the rainfall varies between 60 and 78 inches, and most of it falls in the summer months of December, January, and February. There is very little rain in June, July, and August. There can be disastrously heavy rains—as much as 18 inches have fallen in the city of Santos in one day—but this is rare, and there are few floods except for the regular annual flooding of parts of the Amazon valley.

In the north-eastern bulge there are frequent droughts in the inland areas. As little as 10 inches have fallen in one year in Cabaceiras in the state of Paraíba. In one part of the state of Ceará the average annual rainfall is 18 inches. In sharp contrast is the west of the Amazon valley, where 78 to 116 inches fall in the year; and the extreme north where the rainfall is over 120 inches. In the south, the rain is evenly distributed over the year.

To form a more complete picture of the climatic conditions, it is worth noting the maximum and minimum temperatures of some representative cities as recorded in 1947 (degrees centigrade).

Brazil

City	State	Maximum	Minimum
Pôrto Alegre	Rio Grande do Sul	38·1 ⎫	−1·1 July
Rio de Janeiro	Federal District	37·4 ⎬ January	13·2 July
São Paulo*	São Paulo	34·4 ⎭	4·3 October
Goiânia	Goiás	35·5 ⎫ November	5·8 June & July
Recife†	Pernambuco	31·6 ⎭	19·0 July
Manaus‡	Amazonas	35·5 Sept. & Nov.	21·0 January

*July is consistently the coolest month with a 1947 average minimum of 9·4 against 11·8 for October.
† Readings taken in neighbouring town of Olinda.
‡ In Manaus maximum and minimum daily temperatures vary hardly at all throughout the year.

It is worth noting that the extremes of heat and cold occur in the temperate south. In the greater part of the country the temperature varies much less than anywhere in Europe.

Contrast: Geographic, Economic, and Demographic

GEOGRAPHICAL ZONES

Taking into account all these geographic and climatic factors, Brazil can be divided into several fairly well-defined zones as follows:

(*a*) the south in the temperate zone, with good and well-distributed rainfall and smooth rolling country free of mountain barriers;

(*b*) the coastal plain running from the north of the state of Rio Grande do Sul up to the mouth of the Amazon; well watered and high temperatures;

(*c*) the mountainous area of the south-east, astride the tropic of Capricorn, but sufficiently high to temper the climate; the area of greatest development and densest population;

(*d*) the São Francisco river valley, where many believe the

Brazil

next important economic development of Brazil is to take place;

(*e*) the great central plateau capable of relatively easy development, but as yet sparsely populated and ill provided with communications;

(*f*) the swamp area to the west of the central plateau;

(*g*) the drought areas of the north-east;

(*h*) the vast wet tropical jungle of the Amazon valley.

The wide variety of climatic and geographical conditions makes it possible to produce in Brazil practically any vegetable or animal product known in the world. Cattle, horses, pigs, and poultry nearly everywhere, sheep in the north-east and south, and goats in the north-east; wheat and soft timber in the south; maize, rice, potatoes, coffee, citrus fruit, and all kinds of vegetables in the eastern centre and south; cotton, sugar, and bananas in the eastern centre and north-east, cacao in the north-east, rubber, hardwood, and nuts in the north-east and north, and beans and manioc nearly everywhere; that is the range of Brazilian animal and agricultural production. The relative importance of the various products will be dealt with later.

MINERAL WEALTH

Although Brazil's mineral wealth is almost as great, its range is not so wide and it is not so conveniently distributed. Probably the greatest source of potential wealth is the estimated thirteen thousand million tons of iron-ore deposits, representing between 20 and 25 per cent of the known iron-ore deposits of the world. But these deposits are in the states of Minas Gerais and Mato Grosso, and in the territory of Amapá. They are all difficult to reach, and far from the little coal of not very good quality that is to be found in Brazil only in the states of Rio Grande do Sul, Santa Catarina, Paraná, and, in negligible quantities, São Paulo. Brazil's iron-ore deposits represent enormous wealth once the problems of transport and fuel have been solved; but transport and fuel are in many ways the main problems of Brazil, and it will be a long time before they are substantially solved. Large and unexploited reserves of bauxite are variously estimated at between 120 and 150 million tons.

Brazilian manganese ore deposits may well be the largest in the world, and certainly they have the highest manganese content. Production has amounted to well over 400,000 tons in 1941, but

Contrast: Geographic, Economic, and Demographic
fell to 164,000 tons in 1948. Even so, only the U.S.S.R. and the Gold Coast are bigger producers. As in the case of most of Brazil's other minerals—except for coal and oil—the bulk of the manganese ore deposits are to be found in Minas Gerais.

In a continent abounding in oil, it is strange that so large an area as Brazil should produce so little. Only insignificant quantities have been found so far in the state of Bahia.

Gold is also found in Brazil, and the British owned Morro Velho mine, not far from Belo Horizonte, capital of Minas Gerais, is one of the principal producers. It is one of the world's deepest mines, and has maintained a steady production for well over a century. But Brazil is no longer a gold-exporting country, though gold has played an important part in its history and development.

Precious and semi-precious stones are a valuable product of the country. Diamonds, sapphires, and emeralds, as well as some forty different kinds of semi-precious stones such as aquamarines, tourmalines, amethysts, topazes, and others, are to be found, mostly in Minas Gerais. Diamonds, both for jewellery and for industrial purposes, are often a valuable export; but the value of these exports fluctuates considerably. Exports of precious and semi-precious stones (including quartz crystal) amounted to nearly 215 million cruzeiros in 1946, but were less than 114 million cruzeiros in 1948.

There are several large deposits of phosphates in Brazil, though the only ones now being exploited are those at Jacupiranga in the state of São Paulo. The largest deposits are in the island of Tramira about 200 miles off the coast of the state of Pará; other deposits are in the states of Paraíba, Bahia, and Minas Gerais.

Among other minerals to be found in Brazil are silver, lead, nickel, mica, asbestos, beryllium, tungsten, rutile (titanium), and zirconium. All of these have been exploited to a certain degree but until Brazil develops its industrial activities further, there is considerable risk involved in the mining of these secondary minerals. Demand in world markets fluctuates considerably, and only in time of war can their sale be considered certain.

It is highly improbable that these brief notes sum up the real potential mineral wealth of the country. Vast areas are still unexplored, and of the areas that are already settled, many still await geological surveys; there can be no doubt that many mineral deposits have still to be discovered.

Brazil

It has been seen that in spite of mineral riches, Brazil lacks fuel, and in many ways this has seriously handicapped industrial development. The principal fuel of the non-electrified railways, for example, is wood. But it may well be that in this matter as in so many others, ill fortune will prove ultimately to be an advantage; for Brazil, as will be seen later, is a country which is fortunate even in its misfortunes. The lack of oil and the poor quality and paucity of their coal have made Brazilians conscious of the need to develop electric power. Already by the end of 1948 Brazil had about 2,000 generating plants, of which rather more than half were hydro-electric. It is true that most of these are small, but even so the total capacity amounted to well over a million and a half kilowatts, of which over 85 per cent was obtained from water-power. In addition, hundreds of farmers generate their own electricity from local streams and provide light for themselves and for their workers, as well as power for their agricultural machinery. One of the contrasts of Brazil is the number of labourers whose cottages are built of mud, sometimes thatched and sometimes roofed with rough tiles, and as often as not with packed earth floors, who nevertheless take electric light for granted. In a country as well watered as Brazil there are large potential sources of hydro-electric power. Already many projects of considerable importance have been completed, and many others are now being constructed or have already been planned. These will be referred to later when industrial development is considered.

POPULATION

Even more startling contrasts than those of geography, climate, and subsoil are to be found in the population. The first and most important is the unevenness of its distribution. An examination of statistics shows how small an area of Brazil has been settled, and how much smaller an area has been developed. It is clear that the country could support many times its present population. Its capacity has been variously estimated from a relatively conservative 300 million to an extravagant 700 million. The fact is that except for some parts of the coastal strip and the mountainous area of the south-east, Brazil is under-populated. It must therefore be a source of temptation to any over-populated Power in search of *lebensraum*.

Contrast: Geographic, Economic, and Demographic

The population of Brazil according to the preliminary returns of the last census (end of 1950) was at the time 52,645,479. The following table is based on the 1950 census, and gives a sufficiently accurate picture of the sharp contrasts in the density of population of the various states.

	State	Percentage of Area	Percentage of Population	Population 1950 Census	Density per km.
Densely or moderately well populated states	Alagoas	0·34	2·10	1,106,454	38·78
	Bahia	6·62	9·31	4,900,419	8·70
	Ceará	1·80	5·20	2,735,702	17·85
	Espírito Santo	0·48	1·65	870,987	21·30
	Federal District	0·02	4·58	2,413,152	2,060·76
	Minas Gerais	6·83	14·89	7,839,792	13·47
	Paraíba	0·66	3·29	1,730,784	30·75
	Paraná	2·46	4·08	2,149,509	14·39
	Pernambuco	1·14	6·51	3,430,630	35·36
	Rio Grande do Norte	0·62	1·87	983,572	18·54
	Rio Grande do Sul	3·32	8·00	4,213,316	15·75
	Rio de Janeiro	0·50	4·42	2,326,201	55·83
	São Paulo	2·90	17·56	9,242,610	37·39
	Santa Catarina	1·11	3·00	1,578,159	16·82
	Sergipe	0·25	1·23	650,132	30·87
		29·05	87·69		
Sparsely populated states and territories	Acre	1·80	0·22	116,124	0·76
	Amapá	1·61	0·07	38,374	0·29
	Amazonas	18·74	1·01	530,920	0·33
	Goiás	7·31	2·35	1,234,740	1·98
	Guaporé	2·98	0·07	37,438	0·15
	Maranhão	3·93	3·04	1,600,396	4·82
	Mato Grosso	14·82	1·00	528,451	0·42
	Pará	14·29	2·18	1,142,846	0·96
	Piauí	2·93	2·02	1,064,438	4·27
	Rio Branco	2·52	0·03	17,623	0·08
	TOTAL	70·93	11·99	52,645,479	6·22

NOTE: (1) In the above table the total population figure includes the 162,062 inhabitants of Serra dos Amares, an area in dispute between Minas Gerais and Espírito Santo, not included in the figures for either state. This accounts for the apparent discrepancy in the population percentage.

(2) The figures given above are based on the preliminary returns of the 1950 census. Since then there have been numerous corrections; thus the *Anuário estatístico do Brasil*, 1952, gives two tables showing different totals: 51,944,397 (p. 27) and 52,183,359 (p. 57). The figures quoted are nevertheless sufficiently accurate for the purpose.

13

Brazil

From this table, it is clear that considerably less than a third of the territory of Brazil contains nearly 90 per cent of the population, and that more than two-thirds contains little over 10 per cent. Even after eliminating the inaccessible and so far uninhabitable areas of Amazonas and Mato Grosso, the disparity remains. Brazil includes within its frontiers small zones of the most densely populated areas of the world and enormous tracts of the least populated.

LIVING STANDARDS

Much the same sort of contrasts can be found on examining the standard of living. The great cities of Rio de Janeiro, with more than 2 million inhabitants, and São Paulo, not far behind, offer

Contrast: Geographic, Economic, and Demographic

very high standards. It is true that the income per head of the population is very low, and statistics can be made to show that the standard of living in Brazil is among the lowest in the world. In fact, of course, there are very low standards in some parts of the country; but the statistics are not worth quoting because they give a wholly false picture. The Brazilian needs no fuel to heat his home; he needs relatively few clothes. Those who work in rural areas grow or kill a good proportion of their food; and those

who live in urban centres have standards of living comparable to, though undoubtedly lower than, their opposite numbers in some of the more advanced countries of the world. Certainly they are better off than the people of any other tropical area. But this does not mean that there is not a great disparity between rich

Brazil

and poor. The *favelas*, or tin and scrap-material huts (now being cleared away) on the hilly outskirts of Rio de Janeiro are no pleasant contrast with the luxury homes of Copacabana beach. Nor can the life of the *seringueiro*, or rubber-tapper, be reasonably compared to that of the urban-dweller of the south or centre. To live in one of these centres is to enjoy the amenities of a modern Western city with the added advantage of a mild and equable climate. To live by tapping rubber trees in the Amazon jungle is a very different matter. In his book *The Amazon*,[1] Haakon Mielche has a graphic description of a *seringuero's* home:

> ... a wooden house. This was raised on piles three feet off the ground and its insects. The floor was made of bits of palm, packed more or less closely together. The few windows were mere square holes without glass. They could be shut with palm leaf blinds to keep out the rain. Technically, there were two rooms, though the smaller was really just a corner separated from the rest by some screens. It was a dark corner without a window and here the rubber collector and his wife and the youngest children slept in their hammocks. (Beds they had never heard of). The older children, those who went out to work ... had to hang their hammocks all together in the larger room. There wasn't a chest or a cupboard in the house in which to put anything away. But then, no one had anything to put away. They had no other clothes than those they stood in. The family consisted of six daughters and two sons. It would not be long, however, before there would only be one, as the second was the child with congenital malaria in the head. The wife was small and dreadfully thin. She never stopped coughing and spitting, and seemed to be in the last stages of consumption. ...
>
> A sort of veranda had been built outside the hut. It had a palm leaf roof but no walls. The floor was of flat laths and thin stems, and it dipped and rustled as you walked across it. The gaps in it let you look down into a large muddy pool where pigs grunted and ducks quacked, and through them rose the stench from the garbage which was thrown into it for the pigs and ducks, and from the excrement of the young children who used it as their lavatory. The place was alive with flies and here they had their kitchen.

In this family, Haakon Mielche goes on to say, the parents were wholly illiterate and the elder children could write their names; one of the daughters knew enough clumsily to scrawl the dates of the birth and confirmation of the rest. No one ever washed. Food was all eaten out of the same tin; it was always the same: beans cooked with a bit of fish or bacon rind, or just by themselves and mixed with boiled husked rice and *farofa* (manioc flour) into a thick porridge. They ate with their hands and the food was stirred with sticks.

[1] London, Hodge, 1949, pp. 248–50.

Contrast: Geographic, Economic, and Demographic

This is the sort of problem, to a lesser or even greater degree, that Brazil has to face. Malnutrition and disease undermine the energy and productive capacity of too large a proportion of the population.

There is also the now small number of Indians still in a tribal state and not yet incorporated into the life of the nation. Among these are to be found the Chavante Indians, who are still civilized man's savage enemies and who bitterly and stubbornly resist the encroachment of civilization. But even in the Amazon area the Indians are few. In some Indian tribes were to be found magnificent physical specimens, able to withstand all the perils and diseases of the jungle; but they could not resist the white man's diseases: tuberculosis, and even such apparently mild complaints as measles.

RACIAL ORIGINS

Perhaps this explains why the Indian element in the Brazilian racial composition is relatively so small. Many believe it is smaller than the negro element; it is certainly much smaller than the white. Everything conspires to make difficult any accurate assessment of the racial origins of the Brazilian people. About the aboriginal population there will never be enough information; and though (as will be seen in a later section of this study, on immigration) it is possible to obtain a fairly accurate idea of the numbers of Africans and Europeans who were brought or came into Brazil, this by itself is not enough. In the first place, as has been seen in the introduction, there is no colour bar in Brazil in the sense in which it exists in Anglo-Saxon tropical areas—and of course nothing to compare with the racial hatreds of the south of the United States or of South Africa—and this has led to such a mixture of races that it becomes almost impossible to disentangle them. But while there is no serious racial discrimination or prejudice, there are preferences; there are those who would like to be considered white; there are those who would like to have children whiter than they are themselves; and there are those who will try to pass for white when they are not. Furthermore, there is to be taken into account the so-called 'bleaching' process which began in colonial times when there were practically no white women. The absolute social superiority of the white masters gave them unhampered access to Indian female slaves. It also led to the

Brazil

white men having far more offspring, legitimate and illegitimate, than the men of Indian or negro race. T. Lynn Smith writes on this subject: 'As a result of these factors, the genes of the upperclass white men have not only been passed on to legitimate offspring who have remained at the top of the social pyramid, but they have contributed greatly to the "bleaching" of the darker populations of the lower social strata.'[1]

These and many other considerations and influences have resulted in the white race claiming far more numbers than would appear to be logical or probable on examination of the immigration figures. The *Anuário estatístico do Brasil, 1950* gives the following details of the racial composition of the country based on the 1940 census.

Colour	Total	Percentage of Whole
White	26,171,778	63·46
Black	6,035,869	14·64
Yellow	242,320	0·59
Brown	8,744,365	21·21
Unspecified	41,983	0·10

These figures are probably not very accurate. As the breakdown into sexes and ages gives approximately the same percentages throughout, the 1950 census should reflect the normal process of miscegenation; in other words, a slight increase in the proportion of those classified as brown and a slight decrease in the others. So far returns are available only for the north, north-east, and centre west, and the figures show a much larger increase in the proportion of those classified as brown than could reasonably have been expected in a period of ten years. This probably reflects an increase in the desire not to be black and some diminution in the desire to be white, as well as a real increase in those of mixed race. The number of those returned as black is substantially lower, whereas the number returned as white is only slightly higher and in one region, the north, is lower than in 1940. It seems probable that when the figures for the more populous areas are available they will reveal similar trends.

It has been said that there is no racial prejudice; but this is only relatively true. There are restaurants in the south where negroes would not be served; there are hotels and restaurants in São Paulo and Rio de Janeiro where a coloured man is not often

[1] *Brazil: People and Institutions* (Baton Rouge, Louisiana State University Press, 1946), p. 20.

Contrast: Geographic, Economic, and Demographic

seen; and it is said that a very dark man, or one obviously negroid, is not likely to make much progress in the diplomatic or consular service. But none of this alters the fact that Brazil is by far the most liberal-minded country in this difficult matter. There is reason to suppose that ultimately a fairly homogeneous race will develop in the thickly populated areas of Rio de Janeiro, São Paulo, and Minas Gerais, and undoubtedly it will be predominantly white. In the extreme south, the white element is even stronger; in Bahia the negro element predominates, and in the north-east and north the Indian element is most to be noticed. It remains true to say that the white elements retain their social superiority, but not so much because of their race as because of their education and economic standing.

Much has been said in recent years of Brazil's industrial development; indeed many go as far as to say that today industrial production is higher in value than agricultural production. Statistics can be made to show that this is so; but only by including the value of carcase meat and processed foods under industry. Nor do these figures take into account the considerable production of food in rural areas which is never reflected in official returns. Essentially, for all its industrial advance—and a very impressive advance it has been—Brazil remains an agricultural nation. The heavy concentration of factories in São Paulo is the exception rather than the rule. The new steel plant at Volta Redonda, to which reference will be made later, is still something which, for Brazil, is entirely out of the ordinary.

OCCUPATIONS OF POPULATION

Of the country's man-power, 56·7 per cent is still devoted to agriculture, and only just over 10 per cent to industry, including mining. The following table, though it is based on the 1940 census (the 1950 analysis not yet being available), gives some idea of the occupations of Brazilians. Undoubtedly the new census will show an increase in the percentage of those devoted to industry; but there is no chance of its upsetting the overwhelming preponderance of agriculture.

The growing industrialization has at least one advantage. It is making democracy more nearly possible. It is easier to educate the children of a concentrated group of workers than it is to educate children in sparsely peopled, rural, semi-primitive, and

Brazil

primitive areas. This is not to say that the first result of wider education will necessarily be a political advance; but it does admit of hope for the future. At present, it is probably true to say

Occupation	Men	Percentage	Women	Percentage	Total	Percentage
Agriculture	8,183,313	56·70	1,270,199	8·70	9,453,512	32·56
Industry: manufacturing and mining	1,452,573	10·06	338,043	2·31	1,790,616	6·17
Commerce	746,431	5·17	54,489	0·37	800,920	2·76
Transport and communications	459,758	3·19	13,918	0·10	473,676	1·63
Administration, justice, and State education	227,341	1·57	83,385	0·57	310,726	1·07
Defence and security	170,827	1·18	1,385	0·01	172,212	0·59
Professions, religious activities and private education	78,731	0·55	39,956	0·27	118,687	0·41
Social services and allied services	461,621	3·20	438,153	3·00	899,744	3·10
Domestic activities, school children and students	1,184,239	8·20	10,725,275	73·45	11,909,514	41·01
Balance, including infants	1,469,777	10·18	1,638,435	11·22	3,108,212	10·70

that about half of the population is illiterate. In 1940 the percentage of illiterates above the age of five was 62: the 1950 census gave a corresponding figure of 57 per cent, but many do not learn to read until they are six or seven, or even older. In 1936 about 7 per cent of the total population was enrolled in the primary schools. In 1945, out of an estimated population of 45 million, those enrolled totalled 3,496,664, i.e. nearly 8 per cent. In São Paulo, the most industrialized state, the corresponding estimated percentage is 10½ per cent. These percentages may be compared with the figure for the United States (17½ per cent) or the United Kingdom, where the birth-rate and therefore the proportion of children of school age is much lower (14 per cent).

That, then, is the Brazil of today; a vast land of sharply contrasting climates and geographical conditions; a nation predominantly agricultural but with a thriving and expanding industry; a country that includes unexplored lands peopled by savage tribes as well as some of the biggest and most advanced cities of the world; a people of many origins and yet homogeneous and united. A nation of about 55 million growing at the

Contrast: Geographic, Economic, and Demographic

rate of more than a million a year is clearly destined to play an ever more important role in the world. It was Mr Anthony Eden who said: 'In an increasing manner the voice of Brazil will be heard in the Council of the Nations, which we view with satisfaction.'

CHAPTER II

EXPERIMENT: RACIAL, ECONOMIC, AND POLITICAL

THERE can be no real doubt that the most striking and even possibly the most important experiment in Brazil has been miscegenation. Brazilian sociologists sometimes speak of this experiment as if it had been purposefully carried out. They uniformly speak of it too as a successful experiment. As far as its success is concerned, they are almost certainly right; but it is clear that there was no purpose and that the relative, indeed, as has been seen, almost entire absence of racial prejudice was a matter of accident rather than design. It was a fortunate accident, and one that has undoubtedly saved Brazil a great deal of bitterness and social unrest; but to say it was a fortunate accident does not explain it.

CAUSES OF MISCEGENATION

Many attempts have been made to explain the success of Brazilian miscegenation, and among the most interesting proposals is the theory put forward by Roy Nash and by the Brazilian sociologist Gilberto Freyre. The suggestion is that the Iberian peoples were for centuries used to thinking of a dark-skinned race as masters of a large part of the Iberian peninsula; as social equals if not superiors; and as most efficient agricultural workers. 'Portuguese of the purest Nordic blood', writes Gilberto Freyre, 'had found in brown Moorish women, some of them princesses, the supreme revelation of feminine beauty.'[1] Roy Nash points out that the first contact of the Spaniards and Portuguese with a dark-skinned race was that of the conquered with their conquerors; and he describes the Moors as follows:

The darker man was the more cultured, more learned, more artistic. He lived in the castles and occupied the towns. He was the rich man, and the Portuguese became serfs upon his land. Under such conditions, it would be deemed an honor for the white to marry or mate with the governing class, the brown man, instead of the reverse.[2]

[1] *Brazil: an Interpretation* (New York, Knopf, 1945), p. 19.
[2] *Conquest of Brazil* (New York, Harcourt Brace, 1925), p. 37.

Experiment: Racial, Economic, and Political

Certainly this goes a long way towards explaining why the Iberian peoples have so consistently shown less racial prejudice than any other West Europeans; it explains, too, why in the countries they colonized the aboriginal races are still an important element—and sometimes the dominant one—in the racial composition of the people. The only independent, ex-colonial, and non-Iberian country where the aboriginal race is not either practically eliminated as in Canada, or else held in subjection as in South Africa, is New Zealand. Here the theory put forward by Roy Nash and Gilberto Freyre cannot be applied; but there is another and perhaps a better explanation. The New Zealand Maoris displayed in their dealings with the colonists, both in peace and in war, a standard of courage and of honour fully equal to that of the white man; the Maori became an object of admiration; the noble savage. Maori blood, far from being something to be ashamed of, is a source of pride.

Much the same thing occurred in Brazil. The old and intensely proud aristocracy of São Paulo is essentially the result of the intermarriage between early Portuguese settlers and Indian women. For many of these families, their Indian ancestry is something to boast about. Needless to say, the Indian ancestor is nearly always a brave, powerful, and distinguished chieftain, or else the daughter of a chief—the beautiful and romantic princess. This feeling of pride in Indian ancestry was greatly encouraged when Brazil became independent of Portugal, and as a symbolic gesture of separation many prominent Brazilian families shed their obviously Portuguese names and adopted Amerindian names. But this theory in turn does not explain the toleration shown to negroes and to negro blood in general. The negro was not a noble savage; he was a chattel and a slave; in every way an inferior being. There can be no question of being proud of negro blood, even in Brazil where equally it is not a matter for shame. It is true that among the slaves imported to Brazil there were not a few who had absorbed Mohammedan culture and who read, wrote, and spoke fluent Arabic; men who from every cultural point of view were superior to their masters. But this is not likely to have had a very profound influence, even though it sometimes happened that the daughters of such educated slaves became the mistresses of wealthy or prominent men. It seems more than probable that one of the main reasons for the mixture of races was the fact that the early Portuguese colonist

Brazil

went to Brazil alone, whether he was married or single. In fact, until the period of general European immigration in the late nineteenth century, there was a constant shortage of white women. There was even a period when such white unmarried women as there were in Brazil took to entering religious orders. Man, in Brazil, whether Portuguese immigrant or a Brazilian born of mixed parentage, could not, if he wanted to marry, afford to be too particular—or in fact particular at all—as to the purity of race of the woman he selected to bear his children. Probably miscegenation in Brazil is the result of all these factors, and it is difficult if not impossible to decide which of them exercised the greatest influence.

RACIAL ELEMENTS AND IMMIGRATION

As seen in Chapter I, it is hopeless to attempt to assess the influence on the present racial composition of Brazil of the various factors that have been at work. But the racial elements themselves can be stated. They are:

(a) the Portuguese colonists;
(b) the aboriginal Indians;
(c) the negro slaves imported from Africa;
(d) the late nineteenth and early twentieth century immigrants, especially Italians, Germans, and Poles;
(e) the Japanese immigrants.

Of these, the Portuguese colonists are undoubtedly the strongest influence, an influence constantly strengthened by a continuing though diminished inflow of Portuguese immigrants. The Indian element is important, but nearly always as a result of mating with Portuguese. The *mamelucos*, the offspring of Portuguese settlers and Indian wives, were one of the strongest influences during the colonial period. No one can say just how many negro slaves were imported into Brazil. For many years up to 1830, when the British began to enforce the prohibition of the slave traffic, negro slaves were being imported at the rate of 50,000 a year; another indication of the number of Africans brought into Brazil is an estimate made by Alexander von Humboldt of the population and racial elements of Brazil in 1818:[1]

[1] *Personal Narrative of Travels to the Equinoctial Regions of the New Continent during the years 1799–1804*, tr. H. M. Williams (London, 1814–29), vi. 140–1.

Experiment: Racial, Economic, and Political

Whites	843,000
Negroes	1,887,500
Mixed	628,000
Indians	259,400
Total	3,617,900

The figure given for Indians probably refers only to civilized Indians, and the total almost certainly excludes nearly half a million uncivilized Indians, but it is the proportionately large figure for negroes that is significant. On the other hand, it is estimated that about one-third died and the remainder were discouraged from having children. Some travellers reported that as the males were employed in the fields and the women in household duties, they were rarely together, and Commander Charles Wilkes of the United States navy reported of the years between 1838 and 1842[1] that 'the two sexes are generally locked up at night in separate apartments'. Here undoubtedly was another factor in the 'bleaching' process referred to in Chapter I.

European immigration was encouraged throughout the nineteenth century and the beginning of the twentieth. The severity of British measures against the slave traffic was a powerful stimulus, for Brazilian planters needed workers. Even more important was the abolition of slavery in 1888. European immigrants came pouring in; but not so much to the old plantation areas in the north and in Bahia and Rio de Janeiro, as to the newly opened up lands in São Paulo, Paraná, Minas Gerais, Santa Catarina, and Rio Grande do Sul. Attempts to bring in Chinese coolie labour were frustrated in 1883 by the force of public opinion and by the protests addressed to Peking and to Rio de Janeiro by the British Foreign Secretary, Lord Granville. During this period, therefore, and up to 1908, the only source of new labour in Brazil was European immigration. Some idea of its size and of the states where the immigrants settled can be obtained from the table on page 26.

In 1908 Japanese immigrants began to be admitted, and a total of nearly 200,000 have been allowed to settle. So much have they multiplied that it is estimated that there are now nearly 400,000 people of Japanese origin in Brazil.

[1] *Narrative of the United States Exploring Expedition during the years 1838–42* (New York, Putnam, 1856).

Brazil
Foreign Population of Brazil

State	1872	1890	1900	1920
São Paulo	29,622	75,030	529,187	833,709
Rio Grande do Sul	41,725	34,765	140,854	154,623
Minas Gerais	46,900	46,787	141,647	88,013
Paraná	3,627	5,153	45,134	63,110
Rio de Janeiro	99,899	16,140	57,706	53,770
Santa Catarina	15,974	6,198	32,146	32,138
Mato Grosso	1,669	958	12,205	25,664
Espírito Santo	4,191	3,074	32,936	20,109
TOTAL	243,607	188,105	991,815	1,271,136

(SOURCE: Ministry of Foreign Affairs, *Brazil 1939-40*. Rio de Janeiro, 1940.)

It has been seen how idle it is to pretend that miscegenation in Brazil resulted from any purposeful policy, and how, in fact, it was the product of many circumstances; but Brazilians have not been slow to see the advantages of what their ancestors began. Miscegenation began to be a part of the conscious purpose of many leading Brazilians. Some worked for the assimilation of as yet uncivilized Indians; others to ensure that the European immigrants should be wholly incorporated in the life of the nation. Exclusive foreign clubs and schools, where children were educated to think in a language other than Portuguese and to adhere to foreign standards, have been abolished. Partly no doubt this has been due to fears of what the German community might do during the First World War, and what the Germans, Italians, and Japanese might do in the Second. In the national census of 1940 it was discovered that over a million and a half came from homes where Portuguese was not normally spoken; and of these by far the greater proportion were Brazilian born. The principal languages in use were:

German	644,458
Italian	458,054
Japanese	192,698
Spanish	74,381
Guarani, or other Indian language	58,027

In other words nearly a million and a half people spoke naturally a language other than Portuguese although the number of foreigners in the country was little more than a million and a quarter, and some of these were Portuguese nationals. No figures for the number of foreigners returned in the 1950 census are

Experiment: Racial, Economic, and Political

available for the most heavily populated areas, but from those published so far, a reduction of 10 per cent is probable.

The Brazilian objection to the 1940 situation can be well understood. In any case, as far as miscegenation is concerned, what began as a result of necessity and other factors mentioned has now become a settled policy. But for it, who can doubt that a serious and explosive situation could not have been avoided. Instead of an upper class of decadent whites and a mass of sullen discontented workers there are in Brazil the beginnings of what may yet be a real democracy, and no racial problems for Communism to exploit. In fact, if it is possible to be sure—as indeed it is—that Brazil is to continue to form part of the Western family, and to bring to it as much cultural wealth as it has already begun to do, this is largely because the races are so mixed and racial prejudice is so nearly negligible.

Not unnaturally, Brazilians are eager to combat the views of those who hold that miscegenation leads to deterioration; they have a good case. For no tropical country has shown such purpose, such productive capacity, and such cultural originality as Brazil. None can seriously dispute that the experiment of miscegenation is a success.

EARLY ECONOMIC DEVELOPMENT

Brazilian economic development is in many ways closely tied to the development of the racial composition. The immigration of Portuguese settlers was determined by economic causes. It was the unsatisfactory nature of Indian slave labour that led to the importation of negro slaves. It was the abolition of the slave traffic and the emancipation of slaves that led to the wave of European immigration in the late nineteenth and early twentieth centuries. But Brazil's economic experiments have not been so uniformly successful as the experiment in miscegenation. In general terms, it may be said that Brazil has tried three main experiments, all of which have been successful to begin with; but only the last of them gives signs of ensuring an ultimately prosperous and stable economy. The three experiments are:

(a) the single-agricultural-product plantation economy, which lasted throughout the colonial period and the Empire;
(b) the diversified agricultural economy, which began with the republic;

Brazil

(*c*) the mixed agricultural and industrial economy, which began at about the time of the First World War.

Needless to say, if Brazil's economic development is closely bound up with the development of the racial composition, it is even more bound up with the history of the country. The political aspect of the history is to be dealt with later; but the single-product economy referred to above is, in effect, the history of Brazil's economic development up to the latter part of the nineteenth century.

The difficulty with most history, as the late Philip Guedalla said, is to begin at the beginning; and indeed with most history it is difficult to decide where the beginning really is. However, this is very much less so in the case of Latin America, and is not at all difficult in the case of Brazil. Not much of what happened to the Aztecs, the Chibchas, or the Incas had any real bearing on the history of Mexico, Colombia, or Peru. The history of Spanish America, for all practical purposes, began with the discovery and the conquest. And this is even truer of Brazil, for there was no civilization there comparable to that which the Spaniards found in other parts of the New World: Brazil's history does in fact begin when Pedro Alvares Cabral first sighted the coast of Brazil somewhere about the eleventh latitude south of the equator, in April 1500. And this new land that he discovered, according to the Treaty of Tordesillas, signed some six years earlier, belonged to the crown of Portugal. But Brazil was a disappointment. Portugal was a great navigating and trading state whose sailors had explored the coast of Africa and established trade routes with the Far East. Portuguese interest in the New World arose only because of the wealth that Spain was acquiring; and in fact Portugal had taken relatively very little part in the discovery. Brazil apparently had no gold or silver or precious stones; there were no cities comparable to Tenochtitlán or Cuzco. Portuguese interest in this new possession declined accordingly, and for some time Brazil was little more than a useful place to dispose of criminals and other undesirables. There were of course a few expeditions financed by nobles and in search of gold or silver; but all these came to nothing. Nevertheless, it was at this early stage that the experiment of miscegenation began, and in a few years there were soon to be found large numbers of *mamelucos* who later played so important a part in the development of the colony. In fact, however, Brazil

Experiment: Racial, Economic, and Political

was the Cinderella of the new lands that the Spaniards and Portuguese were discovering. Nevertheless it has been seen already that Brazil is sometimes fortunate in its misfortunes. If Brazil was no El Dorado it did the colony no harm; rather the reverse; for it meant that the settlers and their offspring realized perhaps earlier in Brazil then elsewhere in the New World that wealth could only be acquired by exploiting the natural resources of the country, and by tilling the soil. It meant also, for some time at least, relatively little interference from the metropolis. Indeed, João III of Portugal did not view with any great enthusiasm the need to defend so long a coastline as that of Brazil; he took steps to evade the financial responsibility of this undertaking and divided the known coast of Brazil—roughly from the south of the present state of São Paulo up to the mouth of the Amazon—into twelve (later thirteen) *capitanias*, or hereditary fiefs. Each of them extended some fifty leagues along the coast and far back into the hinterland theoretically up to the line of demarcation laid down in the Treaty of Tordesillas. The holders of these *capitanias* were known as *donatários*, and they had almost sovereign rights, including the right to levy taxes, to raise armies, to enslave Indians, distribute land, and found towns. They did not do well, and some of them even failed in their primary duty of successfully defending themselves against hostile Indians. Perhaps, indeed, their only importance lies in the fact that some of them have been the nuclei of some of the present-day states of Brazil. But what is interesting is what the Portuguese crown expected in return for the rights it gave to the *donatários*. As might be expected, this return was entirely economic; the crown retained the right to levy export duties, the monopoly of Brazil wood, and a fifth of the precious stones and metals that might be discovered. And by this agreement, the crown gave nothing away, for it was Brazil wood that at that time was Brazil's only real source of wealth.

ECONOMIC CYCLES

Red timber—*pau brasil*—gave Brazil its name; its value lay in the dye that could be obtained from it. To begin with it was the only worth-while export and it set the pattern of a one-product economy that Brazil was to follow for nearly four cen-

Brazil

turies. Of course the product was not always *pau brasil*; in fact there was a succession of cycles, each with a different product that boomed and declined. Each cycle had its effect on the nation as a whole; many of them peopled new areas of the country and, even in decline, left behind still another source of wealth. And as each cycle declined, it stimulated activity in other directions, so that today Brazil is less dependent on any one product than at any other time.

Timber provided the first cycle during the sixteenth century, but by the end of it sugar cane had been transplanted from the Cape Verde Islands and had become an important product. Big plantations sprang up and the need for slave labour increased. It was this and the unsuitability of the Indian that led eventually to the importation of negro slaves from Africa. The Indian was nomadic and independent; he did not like labour in the fields. Strangely enough, he could not resist the heat. As late as the middle of the nineteenth century, the British naturalist Henry Bates spoke of the Indian's 'constitutional dislike to the heat'.[1] The negro proved to be a much happier solution, and made Brazil the world's great sugar producer for three centuries. The great plantations—the *engenhos*—with their armies of slaves and their crude cane-crushing machines supplied the Western world with sugar. Even in the early eighteenth century, nearly 150 years after sugar was first commercially grown in Brazil, the value of its annual sugar exports amounted to £3 million sterling—more than Britain's total annual exports at the time. It was overproduction that began to cause planters to turn to other products because of reduced prices, although it was not until the end of the eighteenth century that the development of beet sugar brought the long predominance of sugar cane to an end. Brazil still produces sugar, but exports are negligible; in 1951, for example, sugar exports amounted to less than ¼ per cent of the total value of all exports. However, sugar had done much for Brazil. It had populated and given wealth to the north and north-east; it had made possible the building of cities like Olinda, Recife, and Bahia; and it had accustomed Brazilians to the idea of producing for world markets.

During the predominance of sugar, two other products were developed in the north, tobacco and cacao. Neither of them ever succeeded in taking precedence over sugar, or indeed over any

[1] *The Naturalist on the River Amazon* (London, Murray, 1863), ii. 200–1.

Experiment: Racial, Economic, and Political

of the other products that in turn dominated Brazilian economy; but they made an important contribution to the country's wealth. Up to the end of the eighteenth century Brazil's principal agricultural exports were first, sugar, second, tobacco, and last—a poor third—cacao. Ultimately, the United States and Cuba were to do for tobacco what beet sugar, and to a certain extent Cuba once again, did to cane sugar, and what the Dutch Indies and the Gold Coast have done to cacao; but tobacco and cacao had added to the wealth of the north and north-east, and had begun to accustom the Brazilian planter to think in terms of growing something else besides sugar. In fact, Brazil still produces, and indeed exports, tobacco and cacao.

Meanwhile, still in the eighteenth century and still in the northeast, another product was developed: cotton. Europe suddenly discovered the possibilities of cotton. New machines for spinning and weaving cotton were appearing. England's industrial revolution and the invention of the mechanical loom gave cotton a new value. And so began the experiment of cotton. It was, at any rate to begin with, and before buyers began to be insistent about length of staple and quality, an easy crop to grow; and the Brazilian planter liked an easy crop. Entire plantations that for centuries had produced nothing but sugar were turned over to cotton, and by the early nineteenth century cotton accounted for nearly half Brazil's total exports. Later Mississipi, Georgia, and the Carolinas were to do to the Brazilian cotton trade much the same as Virginia and Cuba had done to the tobacco trade. But though cotton in Brazil suffered a temporary eclipse, it never really died. Later it was cotton that came to the rescue in a desperate economic situation, and in 1948 cotton was Brazil's second largest export. By that time cotton was no longer exclusively grown in the north and north-east. In fact today it is one of the main products of São Paulo and Paraná.

So far all the important economic development of the country had taken place in the north. However, the centre and south were making progress, too, if it was never spectacular and made no fortunes overnight, as in the north and north-east. As far back as 1549, only nine years after Ignatius Loyola founded the order, the Jesuits came to Brazil. Their purpose was not quick wealth but the assimilation of the Indians into Christendom. The Jesuits were a powerful influence for the protection of the Indians, and probably did as much as miscegenation to ensure that the new

Brazil

countries they worked in should not be lost to the indigenous element. Their civilizing work, though less glorious in the eyes of the world than that of the soldiers and planters, had in many ways a more profound influence. The names of the Jesuit fathers, Anchieta and Nóbrega, will always loom large in the history of Brazil, and particularly of São Paulo. In that state the Jesuits established orderly agricultural communities; the Indians were civilized, and they intermarried freely with the Portuguese colonists. It was their offspring, the *mamelucos* who later became the scourge of the Indians, but who in fact were responsible for opening up Brazil's vast interior.

Even before the settlement of Brazil, the Portuguese had negro slaves; nevertheless, during the first two centuries of the colony relatively few were brought over to Brazil. During the first century the Indians provided all the necessary labour, but later, as the big sugar estates came to be developed, and as the Jesuits continually worked to protect the Indian from slavery, the shortage of labour became acute, and war with Holland prevented any large-scale importation of Africans. It was then that the *mamelucos* from São Paulo broke away from the ordered communities set up by the Jesuits and accompanied by numerous slaves and *agregados*, these Paulista *bandeirantes*, as they came to be called, set off on long exploring and Indian-hunting expeditions; they were resolute and ruthless, and not satisfied with enslaving the Indians they captured as a result of their skirmishes with tribes in the interior, they raided and enslaved the Indians who had already been civilized and were living peaceably in settlements set up and administered by religious communities. At the same time, the *bandeirantes* took with them their cattle, and drove their herds throughout all the accessible parts of Brazil. They advanced to the south through Paraná and Santa Catarina, and they pushed on into the pampas of Rio Grande do Sul. They went west into Mato Grosso, and even north-west into Goiás; to the north and east they went to Minas Gerais, down the valley of the São Francisco and out into the *sertão* (hinterland) beyond the state of Bahia, in the hinterland of Pernambuco, Ceará, Piauí, and Maranhão. Wherever they went they took with them their cattle, and they appropriated huge tracts of land for cattle-raising purposes. Everywhere, too, they established small settlements based on this cattle economy.

Thus it was that peaceful Jesuits and lawless *bandeirantes* be-

Experiment: Racial, Economic, and Political

tween them provided some sort of solid economic background for the fluctuating prosperity of the coastal regions of the north-east and the north. The agriculture of São Paulo and the cattle of the south, the São Francisco valley and the *sertão*, constituted the earliest beginning of the more diversified agricultural economy which was to be Brazil's next experiment.

In 1700 still another event occurred to upset the economic dominance of the north; gold was discovered in Minas Gerais; and this, too, must be attributed to the *bandeirantes*. The news of this discovery—to which was added the discovery of diamonds—had a profound effect and produced the wildest excitement. Unsuccessful planters and poor immigrants rushed in from the coast. Before the authorities could establish law and order, pitched battles were fought between the Paulistas and the gold-seekers from Portugal and other parts of Brazil. In a short while the exploitation of gold was in full swing: big cities mushroomed into existence, such as Villa Real and Villa Rica, now known as Ouro Preto. More gold was produced in fifty years than was obtained from the whole of the rest of America until the discovery of Californian gold; but by 1770 the alluvial gold was exhausted. The rich veins from which it must have come are hard to find and even harder to work. It has been seen already that the British-owned mine in Morro Velho is one of the deepest mines in the world. Ouro Preto had begun to decay, and still another cycle, though not an agricultural one, had ended. Nevertheless a new state had been opened up—one of the richest and best populated in the country. Minas Gerais had in effect been added to the colony: and Brazil still produces gold, though it is no longer exported.

Meanwhile the cycle of cotton in the north and north-east was not yet exhausted. And it was while cotton was still dominant that coffee was born in the early nineteenth century.

The taste for coffee began to spread over Europe and North America, and in a very few years Brazil had a virtual monopoly which was retained until the beginning of the present century; by then the more delicate types, from Colombia and Central America, began seriously to compete even at a higher price. In the second half of the last century coffee became Brazil's largest export: it remains so to this day. But during the 1920s and 1930s again over-production brought the price down. World economic slumps were quickly reflected in the sale of any product not

Brazil

absolutely essential. Brazil became as famous for burning coffee and throwing it into the sea as it had been for producing it. Nevertheless prices were not kept up, or at least not sufficiently, and it was at this stage that Brazil's second experiment of a diversified agricultural economy really began to bear fruit. Cotton once again became an important product; but not in the north, and not haphazardly as in the past. It was in São Paulo that it was now grown, efficiently, scientifically, and competitively. However, the production of coffee was not discontinued; on the contrary, it is still a great source of wealth; and the state of São Paulo has become the wealthiest and most populated of Brazil. Not only that, but combined with the neighbouring state of Minas Gerais, the second most populated in the country, and Rio de Janeiro, State and Federal District, there has grown up in this south-eastern area of Brazil a sufficient concentration of population (a total of 21,821,755 in 1950) to provide a home market of sufficient size for the nascent industries of the country. It is that which has made possible Brazil's third economic experiment: a mixed agricultural and industrial economy.

One more cycle must be noted before passing on to the early political story of Brazil, the cycle of rubber. The story begins and ends during the predominance of coffee. During the nineteenth century, the industrial world discovered the use of rubber. Towards the end of the century and at the beginning of the twentieth, tyres for motor cars and cycles called for large amounts of rubber. For a long time rubber could be obtained only from *Hevea brasiliensis*, a tree which grew only in Brazil. At the end of the century Brazil had a virtual monopoly of rubber, and a new part of the country—the Amazon—had begun to be developed. The port of Belém, capital of Pará, acquired a new importance; and Manaus, capital of the state of Amazonas and over 1,000 miles up the Amazon, was built on the wealth of rubber. The prosperity of Manaus during the boom years is proverbial; the building of one of the finest opera houses in the world and the magnificent palaces of the rubber millionaires were headline news. But Brazil's monopoly of rubber was short-lived; for an enterprising young Englishman smuggled a few seeds or seedlings out of Brazil. They reached Kew Gardens where they thrived in artificial conditions, and within a very few years seedlings were sent to Malaya and Ceylon, to Java and Sumatra, where new scientific plantations were soon producing rubber of better quality

Experiment: Racial, Economic, and Political

and at a competitive price. Very few figures are necessary to show how the Brazilian rubber boom came to an end. Whereas in 1900 Brazilian exports are estimated to have been rather less than 30,000 tons, and Asian production a purely experimental 4 tons, by 1912 Asian production of 45,000 tons was already higher than Brazilian rubber exports for that year. In 1930 Brazilian exports were about 14,000 tons as compared to over 800,000 produced in Asia. Brazil still produces rubber, however, and Amazonas has begun to be peopled.

That, briefly, is the early economic history of Brazil, from the first beginnings, through the period of the single-product agricultural economy, until the beginning of industrialization. In a sense, the industrialization of Brazil is as much an experiment, and certainly a more conscious one, as any other Brazilian economic development, but it can be considered more properly as part of the emancipation of the country, and will therefore be examined in the next chapter.

EARLY POLITICAL HISTORY TO 1822

The political history of Brazil, too, is at once experiment and emancipation, although the emancipation of the people did not begin in any real sense until after the abolition of slavery in 1888 and the declaration of the republic in 1889.

Throughout the history of the colony, Brazil suffered and benefited from the weakness of the mother country. From 1580 until 1640 Portugal was united with Spain, and Portuguese possessions were exposed to attacks from the enemies of Spain. From 1640 until 1668 Portugal was engaged in a war of liberation from Spain, which was eventually successful; but in order to achieve that success, Portugal had to make important concessions in the matter of trade to France, Holland, and above all to Britain The American historian J. F. Rippy goes as far as to say that Portugal and its American colony became the economic vassals of Britain.[1] Certainly it is true that by 1700, not quite half the trade of Brazil was in the hands of the British, and that during the eighteenth century this predominance increased. But Portugal's troubles did not lead only to inroads into and the final breakdown of its monopoly of Brazilian trade; they led also to armed

[1] *Historical Evolution of Hispanic America*, 3rd ed. rev. (New York, Crofts, 1945), pp. 116-19.

Brazil

attacks against the colony, of which the most noteworthy were those of the French and Dutch. In 1594, as the result of a landing in Maranhão by the French pirate, Jacques Rifault, trade began between that captaincy and the port of Dieppe. Daniel de la Touche was granted a concession in the area by Henry IV of France, which after his death was renewed by the queen regent. In 1612, he set up the fort and colony of Saint Louis, and from there began exploring the region; but by 1615 the Brazilian colonists had driven the French back into Guiana. In 1710 the French tried again. A first attack on Rio de Janeiro failed, but a year later the French seized the city, sacked it, and held it to ransom. They won great booty but did not attack again.

The Dutch were more purposeful and, for a time, more successful. In 1624 they captured Bahia but were able to hold it for less than a year. In 1630 they took Recife and Olinda, and from those cities gradually extended their influence over northern Brazil. Prince Maurice of Nassau, the governor of the Dutch settlement, was an able administrator and the Dutch colony prospered; the Dutch West India Company profited, but after some fourteen years of prosperity tried to increase its profits still further. The Portuguese settlers began to revolt, and by 1645 the whole population, including the *mamelucos*, Indians, and negroes, were in arms against the Dutch; the invaders were finally driven out in 1654.

In spite of all these troubles Brazil prospered. It suffered very much less from restrictions imposed by the metropolis than did the Spanish American colonies, not so much because the Portuguese were not mercantilists, but because they were not in a position to enforce to the full the restrictions that the mercantile theory implied. Brazil accordingly benefited, and from 1661 agents of British and French merchant houses were allowed to establish themselves in Recife, Bahia, and Rio de Janeiro. But there were restrictions, and among the more burdensome were the high price of salt and the limitations on manufacturing and food processing. The former was keenly felt by the cattle raisers, who needed salt to preserve their meat, and the latter prevented the manufacture of any article made from cotton, flax, or silk, and of any gold or silver work; it also prevented the refining of sugar, and reserved a good part of the tobacco crop for Portuguese factories. This prevention of manufacturing—an integral part of the mercantile theory—is a characteristic of colonial

Experiment: Racial, Economic, and Political

economies, and no ex-colonial territory believes itself to have achieved emancipation until it has gone some way in the direction of industrialization; it probably still is a psychological factor in the enthusiasm with which Brazil has turned to industry in recent times.

During the greater part of the colonial period the political organization remained more or less as it was when first laid down by João III in the second quarter of the sixteenth century. The number of captaincies increased, and their prosperity varied greatly. Governors-General were installed first in Bahia and later in Rio de Janeiro as well. From 1640 Brazil became a viceroyalty, and the viceregal capital was Bahia. In spite of these arrangements the central authority over the captaincies was largely nominal, and the chief executives of the captaincies retained a large measure of their nearly sovereign powers. Abuses there undoubtedly were, but the absence of centralization had beneficial effects. Each captaincy was enabled to develop along its own lines without hampering and uniform restrictions from the centre, of the type that were so common in Spanish American colonies; and there can be no doubt that the colonists preferred it so. They probably looked upon it as a great misfortune when the Marquis of Pombal, who controlled the Portuguese government from 1750 until 1777, introduced drastic reforms and centralized the administration of the Colony. However, this is another example of a misfortune that ultimately proved fortunate. The unification of the administration of Brazil increased the homogeneity of the colony already begun by the *bandeirantes*, and it is probably true to say that those two factors have done more than anything else to spare Brazil the bitter and costly fratricidal struggles that rent the Spanish American colonies when, in the early nineteenth century, they achieved their independence.

In 1763 the capital was transferred from Bahia to Rio de Janeiro, and the capital at last acquired real authority over the colony. Pombal brought to an end the captaincies and annulled the ancient rights of the *donatários*; he unified the administrative system and for the first time employed Brazilian-born officials in civil posts, and allowed Brazilians to become officers in the army; he did much for agriculture and even promoted industries where these did not affect the industries of Portugal. It was Pombal, too, who finally declared in 1755 that the Indians were free citizens of the colony and could not therefore be enslaved; in this way he

Brazil

avoided the possible ill-treatment of the Indians that might have resulted from his expulsion of the Jesuits.

During this period, except for a small minority, little attention was paid to culture, the arts, or to education in general. Such schools as there were, were nearly all set up by religious orders, and an effort to found a university in Rio de Janeiro in 1776 ended in failure. This perhaps was the penalty of the many years during which the captaincies were virtually independent of the centre. In Spanish America the viceregal capitals of Lima, Mexico, and Bogotá were sufficiently large centres, and concentrated enough wealth, to make possible the early foundation of universities. Nevertheless, there were educated classes in Brazil, and not a few Brazilian-born students were to be found in the University of Coimbra. In addition, English and French works were included in the libraries of rich men's houses. The new ideas abroad in Europe were not excluded from Brazil, and, for example, at the time of the French Revolution, in 1789, Tiradentes, or to give him his proper name, Joaquim José da Silva Xavier, now a national hero, tried to bring about a republic in which there should be freedom of thought and of industry, no monopolies and no slavery.

It was at the beginning of the nineteenth century that, once again in the guise of misfortune, Brazil experienced one of her greatest strokes of fortune. At about the same time when, in the rest of South America, the long struggles for independence were beginning, which ended with the triumphant success of the two liberators, Bolívar and San Martín, and the final defeat of the Spaniards in December of 1824 at Ayacucho, Napoleon's troops invaded Portugal. The Portuguese were in no way able to resist the experienced French soldiers. To avoid falling into captivity the Prince Regent, Dom João (the future João VI), and the royal family, together with as many courtiers as were able to, sailed for Brazil under the protection of the British fleet. The Regent was received enthusiastically in Rio de Janeiro, and in 1808 decreed a number of reforms. The first printing press was set up, new educational centres were established, a supreme court and other tribunals were created, foreign scientists and settlers were welcomed, and the trade of Brazil was thrown open to all nations. When in 1816 Dom João's mother died, he assumed the style of João VI of the 'United Kingdom of Portugal, Brazil, and the Algarves'; in spite of occasional liberal or republican risings

Experiment: Racial, Economic, and Political

Brazil prospered in peace, and the people grew used to being citizens of a sovereign nation instead of colonists subject to the will of a metropolitan country. Finally, in 1821, Dom João VI returned to Portugal at the request of the Portuguese provisional government, and he left behind as regent of Brazil—no longer viceroy—his son Pedro.

In Lisbon, however, the re-established Portuguese government viewed with no satisfaction the new status and prerogatives of their erstwhile colony. Ideas of a return to mercantilism and even of a restoration of the captaincies were seriously entertained, and the Regent Pedro was ordered to return home. This he refused to do; and finally on 7 September 1822, he pronounced the famous 'Grito de Ypiranga'; 'Comrades, the Cortes of Portugal wants to reduce Brazil to slavery; we must declare forthwith her independence . . . Independence or death!'

POLITICAL HISTORY: THE EMPIRE (1822–89)

On 12 October, Dom Pedro I became Emperor of an independent Brazil. Thus a chain of accidental and apparently unfortunate accidents gave Brazil independence without the bloodshed that occurred elsewhere in Latin America. Dom Pedro was able to deal with such reactionaries and Portuguese troops as opposed him, as also with the republicans of Pernambuco, but he was obliged in 1824 to grant a fairly liberal Constitution, in which nevertheless the crown retained the so-called moderative power. An elected lower house and a senate selected by the Emperor; ministers and a council of state appointed by the Emperor; and imperial power to convoke or dissolve the Chamber of Deputies and to suspend any acts of the legislature; these were the main points of the Constitution that lasted nearly sixty years. It also guaranteed freedom of speech and of the press, equality of citizens before the law, and a fair measure of religious toleration.

Dom Pedro I was not a successful monarch. Circumstances were against him. Republican feeling was strong, and there were many risings; he was involved in a war with Argentina over the Banda Oriental; to bring hostilities to an end and allow the resumption of trade Britain intervened, and the independent republic of Uruguay was created. The Emperor rapidly lost popularity, and when finally he lost the support of the army in 1831, he abdicated in favour of his young son Pedro.

Brazil

For nine years various regencies ruled Brazil in increasing disorder. Among the worst troubles was the revolt of Rio Grande do Sul which was not finally crushed until 1845; but there were many other factors, in particular the conflicting aims of the liberal monarchists, the conservatives, and the federalists. Eventually, at the age of fourteen, Dom Pedro II took over the reins of government, as a result of a persistent liberal campaign, in July of 1840.

Dom Pedro II proved to be an able ruler; in many ways the most successful Brazil has ever had, even though his reign ended with the proclamation of the republic and with the exile of himself and his family. He was a man of taste and culture, with progressive ideas and a keen interest in scientific ideas; he had liberal principles and was democratic to a degree in his manners and habits; nevertheless, he believed that the function of a ruler was to rule, and he never hesitated to exercise the 'moderative' power reserved for the crown by the Constitution. It was Dom Pedro who accustomed Brazil to the idea that opposing political parties could peacefully succeed each other in office; and to the essentials of a two-party system. It was he who pacified the country in the earlier years of his reign and brought to an end the revolt of Rio Grande do Sul, suppressed risings in other parts of the country, and assured internal peace. He fought two wars, one against the tyrant Rosas of Argentina in 1852 and 1853, and the other against the dictator López of Paraguay, from 1864 to 1870.

Dom Pedro's enlightenment manifested itself in other ways. He encouraged foreign trade, which was four and a half times as great in value at the end of his reign as it was at the beginning; he also favoured the acceptance of immigrants and in 1888, for example, as many as 131,000 entered the country through the ports of Rio de Janeiro and Santos; he encouraged the building of railways and telegraph communications; and during his reign the population doubled. Education did not make as much progress, and the percentage of illiterates was still ninety at the end of Pedro's reign. Nevertheless, there were some cultural developments in music, sculpture, architecture, and letters. It was during this period that Brazil was consolidated as one of the nations of the Western civilization and way of life. Abroad, and in foreign relations, the emperor was respected as an enlightened monarch. His visits to the United States, England, France, and Italy evoked widespread interest and enthusiasm.

Nor was Dom Pedro illiberal in his policy in regard to the

Experiment: Racial, Economic, and Political

problem of slavery. The slave trade was officially abolished before he took command, but it continued in a reduced form until 1853, when it is estimated that there were nearly 3 million slaves in Brazil. By 1870 there were less than 2 million, and in 1871 was passed the law of *ventre livre*, by which all children of slave mothers were born free. In 1888 there were less than three-quarters of a million slaves, and in spite of the liberal attitude of the crown, the big planters and landowners looked to the monarchy as the stabilizing influence that would ensure their retaining their depleted labour force. And though Dom Pedro had offended the army by his pacifist sympathies, and was on bad terms with the Church through refusing to expel freemasons, his personal popularity, combined with the support of the landowners, seemed enough to guarantee the stability of the throne. Nevertheless the aristocracy resented the paternal, almost tutorial rule of Dom Pedro; and, in addition, the Emperor failed to understand or give enough importance to the rising professional classes that his own rule had made possible. Trouble came when Dom Pedro was in Europe, lying ill in Milan; his daughter, Princess Isabella, acting as regent in the Emperor's absence, abolished slavery without compensation for the slave owners. The throne lost its last influential pillar of support, and even its popularity was on the wane, not on account of the now ageing Emperor but because of the insolent and haughty manners of the Count d'Eu, the French husband of Princess Isabella. A revolt led by Benjamin Constant Botelho de Magalhães, a professor of mathematics, and General Deodoro da Fonseca, broke out on 15 November 1889; and on the following day the Emperor was deposed, and he and his family banished.

CHAPTER III

EMANCIPATION: POLITICAL, ECONOMIC, AND CULTURAL

POLITICAL HISTORY: THE REPUBLIC (1889-1932)

IN many ways the proclamation of the republic in 1889 marks the most important step in the emancipation of Brazil from her original colonial status. But this emancipation in Brazil was, as everywhere, a gradual process. Even the declaration of independence in 1822 was the result of a gradual process: the spread among the educated classes of new ideas from Europe, and the example of the United States. Similarly, the proclamation of the republic was in line with new ideas and new economic forces. Even if the empire had not fallen, Brazil seemed to be entering upon a new era of prosperity. At the beginning of the century, when under Dom João VI Brazil was freed from the economic control of Portugal, it did not, as we have seen, by any means lose its colonial economic status. Its products continued to be sold mainly in European markets, and though the general tendency was for the price of these products to rise, the improvement did not keep pace with the rising standards of living of the people. In fact, the need for imports outstripped the capacity for exports. As a result, Brazil for years had an adverse balance of trade that could only be rectified by means of loans from abroad; loans which were mostly negotiated in London. Much the same problem was experienced in the United States, but there the problem was more easily solved. Loans were necessary there, too, for railway construction and other enterprises; and on these loans there was eventually a good deal of defaulting. But the real solution in the United States was the development of industry. For reasons that have already been touched on—and that will be examined more closely later—this solution was not possible in Brazil. One reason for this apparent lack of enterprise was the fact that Dom João VI was compelled to sign a commercial treaty with Britain by which customs duties on British goods were reduced to 15 per cent. Political pressure compelled Brazil to grant the same terms to most of the manufacturing countries, and it was therefore obliged

Emancipation: Political, Economic, and Cultural

to maintain what was, in effect, a free-trade policy. The industries of the United States were built up behind the protection of high tariff walls. With a small potential market, and in the face of competition from efficient British manufacturers, no Brazilian industrial enterprise could hope to achieve much success; and this situation lasted until 1844. Tariffs were eventually raised, but by that time Brazil was a long way behind in industrial technology.

It was not until the development of coffee, mainly, in the early stages, in the Paraíba valley in the state of Rio de Janeiro (between the Serra do Mar and the Serra da Mantiqueira) that Brazil began to enjoy a substantial favourable balance of trade. In addition, the arrival of large numbers of European immigrants brought new life and energy. Brazil was ready for a period of expansion. In a sense, the final abolition of slavery and the fall of the empire were symbolic of the new stirring of the nation: the desire to cut adrift from the past and to make of Brazil a modern Western nation. In spite of the experience gained under the empire, however, the art of politics did not come easily to the Brazilians, and the early days of the republic were marked by many troubles.

The young republic's new Constitution was produced in February 1891. It was modelled largely on the Constitution of the United States, with an upper house of senators, a lower house of deputies, and a presidential executive without a Prime Minister. It was a federal Constitution and the states kept a great many of their rights; nevertheless, the federal government was entitled to intervene in a number of circumstances, and this right has been freely made use of. The Constitution also contained a bill of rights by which were ensured freedom of speech and of the press, trial by jury, religious toleration, the abolition of the death penalty, the separation of church and state, the civil state of marriage, and the secularization of education.

General Deodoro da Fonseca, who had been chief executive of the provisional government, was the first president, but he proved to be so inefficient, tactless, and dictatorial that before the end of the year he was compelled to resign in favour of the vice-president, Floriano Peixoto, who later became a Marshal of the army. He, too, proved to be unsatisfactory, and his administration was marked by a naval revolt which spread to Rio Grande do Sul and cost many lives and eight months of fighting before it was finally suppressed. It looked as if Brazil was going the way of so

Brazil

many of her sister republics of Latin America: internecine strife with military *caudillos* and real power in the hands of the armed forces. It was indeed feared, when in the presidential campaign a São Paulo lawyer—Prudente José de Moraes Barros—was elected, that Peixoto would refuse to hand over the government of the country when his term of office expired. Fortunately for Brazil this did not happen, and a civilian president took over.

It is worth noting that the army in Brazil is not characterized by the upper-class conservative tradition common to the armies of so many countries. Though the Brazilian army has had too great an influence in politics, it is surprising that as often as not this influence has been thrown against a ruler with absolutist tendencies. In any case, the new president, Prudente José de Moraes Barros, took firm steps to reduce the military influence in the government and replaced many officers who had been appointed to civilian posts. But he too was compelled to put down many uprisings, and was faced with a serious financial crisis at the end of his term. This was the main problem of his successor, Manoel de Campos Salles, another Paulista elected partly through the aid of his predecessor and in opposition to a militarist candidate. The financial crisis was solved in the classical way by means of negotiating a loan for £10 million with the Rothschilds.

Rodrígues Alves, who became president in 1902, was the third successive Paulista to hold presidential office. It was largely due to him, to Pereira Passos, prefect of Rio de Janeiro, and to Dr Oswaldo Cruz, who fought a successful war against mosquitoes and stamped out yellow fever, that Rio was converted into a modern capital, well laid out, with fine buildings and a good health record. But this achievement did not lessen the jealousy of the other states of Brazil. In the next presidential campaign they combined together to break the monopoly of the presidency that São Paulo seemed to be acquiring. Afonso Augusto Moreira Penna was a Mineiro from the state of Minas Gerais. His main task was a successful overhaul of the nation's finances and the establishment of a national bank. Penna died before the end of his term of office and was followed for a short period by the vice-president, Nilo Peçanha.

In 1910 the conservatives made a determined assault on the presidency. They gained the support on this occasion of the army by the simple expedient of selecting as their candidate the nephew of Deodoro da Fonseca, Marshal Hermes da Fonseca. The out-

Emancipation: Political, Economic, and Cultural

going President Peçanha supported the Marshal, who won the election against the liberals, led by their candidate Ruy Barbosa. The liberals alleged electoral fraud and challenged the validity of the decision; shortly after Hermes da Fonseca took office the navy revolted and there was serious bloodshed. Some of the leaders of the revolt were shot, and the city of Bahia (São Salvador) Barbosa's birthplace, was bombarded. Barbosa and his liberal supporters prepared themselves for a vigorous campaign in the next elections, but in order to avoid possible bloodshed and the inevitable bitterness of such a campaign, at a time when Brazil's economic position was once again in a state of crisis, Barbosa withdrew in favour of Wenceslau Braz, a politician from the state of Minas Gerais. Brazil at that time was suffering from the heavy fall in the price of coffee and from the fierce competition of the Far East in the rubber market. Barbosa's statesmanship resulted in the election of Wenceslau Braz.

The republic had been in existence for a quarter of a century, and Brazil had made much progress, but it was during the administration of Braz that Brazil really took its place among the more important nations of the world. Growing industrialization made great strides, and in spite of war-time difficulties, by 1918 the country was enjoying a period of prosperity. Braz was succeeded by a Paulista, ex-president Rodrígues Alves, but he was too ill to discharge his duties. The vice-president assumed office until Epitácio da Silva Pessôa, from the state of Paraíba, was elected president for the remainder of the presidential term of office. Under him Brazil faced the post-war depression, and great hardship was caused by the rising cost of living. Nevertheless the administration did much for the drought-afflicted areas of the north-east by building dams and storing water.

Although Pessôa was from Paraíba, the victor of the 1918 election had been a Paulista; and he was preceded by Braz, a Mineiro. A new political pattern had begun to be accepted, by which the presidency fell alternately to a Mineiro and a Paulista. It caused no surprise, therefore, when, with the aid of the outgoing president, Artur Bernardes from Minas Gerais was elected to take office in 1922. His election, however, aroused intense opposition among the military and civilian supporters of the unsuccessful opposition candidate, ex-president Nilo Peçanha. Violence and fraud were alleged, and there were numerous military uprisings in which the leaders were sometimes self-seeking but sometimes

Brazil

quite genuinely and idealistically attacking what they believed to be a corrupt oligarchy. And indeed it must be admitted that presidential elections could scarcely be said really to reflect the democratic will of the people. The vast majority of the rural masses were hardly politically conscious and far from being mature. The electoral franchise was limited, and the possibility of manipulating the elections was far too great. In the rural areas particularly the owners of the great *fazendas* had only to instruct their workers to vote one way or another. The fact remains that even before Bernardes took office there was serious trouble in Rio de Janeiro, and later, when Bernardes was already installed, there were military revolts in São Paulo and in Rio Grande do Sul. During practically the whole of the presidency of Bernardes the republic was in a state of siege, and the administration was able to carry out only a part of its programme of economic and social reform.

As might have been expected, Bernardes was succeeded by a Paulista, Washington Luis Pereira de Souza, who showed himself to be an energetic and capable administrator. He pacified the country and ended the state of siege in 1927. He was conscious of one of Brazil's greatest handicaps—lack of transport facilities— and set on foot an ambitious road-building programme. He was also active in the marketing of coffee and in financial problems. But he was unable to prevent the great depression that began in 1929. Every one of Brazil's now numerous agricultural commodities slumped on the world's markets; and the break on the coffee market was in itself disastrous. There followed every sort of economic and political consequence. Economically, it was a serious setback to the rising national industry, and an even heavier blow to agriculture; there were many bankruptcies and much unemployment. The political consequences were much influenced by the fact that the President, himself a Paulista, instead of backing a Mineiro as the unwritten agreement demanded, supported a fellow Paulista, Júlio Prestes, and so split the official government supporters. For the Mineiros bitterly resented what they considered a betrayal and they hastily looked for friends elsewhere; they found them in João Pessôa, governor of Paraíba in the north, and Getúlio Vargas, governor of Rio Grande do Sul in the south. The latter became the candidate of the new alliance, the so-called Aliança Liberal. When Vargas was defeated, not many believed the elections to have been fairly carried out. Certainly his sup-

Emancipation: Political, Economic, and Cultural

porters did not; and revolution followed, a revolution in which the army largely supported Vargas and in which he was undoubtedly aided by the serious economic plight of the nation. It was in fact practically a bloodless revolution, and it ended in November 1930 with Getúlio Vargas installed in the presidential Catete Palace in Rio de Janeiro, and his close friend and supporter, Oswaldo Aranha, as Minister of Justice and Internal Affairs. The long presidential reign of Getúlio Vargas had begun.

It was not to be supposed that the Paulistas would welcome this turn of events, or that they would accept the situation. In 1932 they duly revolted. Vargas, on taking over the presidency, had promised a prompt return to constitutional government, and the Paulistas felt that two years was long enough to wait. They labelled their revolt Constitucionalista. It looked to be the most serious internal struggle that Brazil had ever suffered; enthusiasm in São Paulo ran high; support from the industrial and moneyed classes was considerable. But it did not last; within a few months the rebel forces had disintegrated or surrendered; the leaders fled or were imprisoned. The president showed great wisdom and magnanimity; there was a complete amnesty for members of the revolutionary army, and Getúlio Vargas was more firmly entrenched than ever. He remained in office until after the end of the Second World War, and there was internal peace in the country, except for an abortive Communist revolution in 1934, and an equally unsuccessful Integralista revolt in 1937, throughout that period. But Getúlio Vargas, who was elected president by popular suffrage for the first time (1950), belongs really to the present rather than to the past. His first term of office will be dealt with in a later chapter.

INDUSTRIAL DEVELOPMENT

It is time now to turn to Brazil's economic development, to what may fairly be called her economic emancipation. The story hinges largely on industrialization, and it is the development of Brazil's industry that must be considered first.

In his brief study of the growth of industry in Brazil,[1] Roberto Simonsen poses the question of why Brazil did not develop in-

[1] *Brazil's Industrial Revolution* (São Paulo, Escola Livre de Sociología e Política, 1939).

Brazil

dustrially on lines similar to the United States; he asks himself why it is that the United States has become so economically powerful—so much more so than Brazil—when in 1776, when the United States became independent, its exports barely reached £1 million, while Brazil's production was such that it could and did export more than three times as much. Furthermore, it must be borne in mind that at that time the colony was already in possession of almost all its present territory (the territory of Acre has been the only substantial addition) whereas the United States then occupied but one-sixth, increased a century later to two-thirds, of its present territory. Why then, asked Roberto Simonsen in 1939, is the industrial output of the United States a hundred times larger than that of Brazil?

One of the reasons has already been referred to at the beginning of this chapter, Brazil's inability for the first half of the nineteenth century to set up a high protective tariff wall. Undoubtedly this had some influence, but it is possible to exaggerate it. The extraordinary expansion of the United States would not have been possible without the development of heavy industry; without in fact a high production of iron and steel. Nor would it have been possible without fuel; furthermore, the iron ore and the fuel—in other words the coal—had to be reasonably near each other. Other sources of energy and power have also aided industrial development in the United States—hydro-electricity and oil. In addition, European immigration into the United States has been very large indeed (far higher than immigration into Brazil), and the climate is in the main healthy and invigorating. This provided at once the man-power and an internal market of sufficient size to justify and make profitable internal industrial development. The larger part of the territory of the United States is wholly suitable for human habitation and is free from mosquito-borne plagues like malaria and yellow-fever. Finally the geography of the United States made railway construction comparatively easy. Very different is the picture presented by Brazil. As has been seen already, in Chapter I, although there are enormous iron-ore deposits, they are inconveniently placed; they are far from what little coal, and that of inferior quality, Brazil possesses. Hydro-electric power is now being produced, but oil, in spite of many tenaciously held hopes, has not yet been discovered in any substantial quantity. Nor is the climate as invigorating and healthy as that of the United States; nor has the influx of immigrant

Emancipation: Political, Economic, and Cultural

energy been anything like so great. Furthermore, Brazil's jungles and rivers, as well as her mountains, have been a serious obstacle to the development of communications. In fact, it is not so much the tardiness of Brazilian industrial development that is a cause for wonder, as the energy and drive that are now being displayed and the speed with which Brazil is catching up.

It is nearly a century and a half since Dom João VI first tried to sponsor industrial development in the colony after centuries of mercantilist suppression; but he was not very successful, and no significant progress was made. From 1850 until 1870 much more determined efforts were made by Irineu Evangelista de Souza, Viscount of Mauá. Already the more serious effects of the near free-trade policy had been removed, although a frankly protectionist policy was not adopted until 1888. Mauá and his friends did everything they could to promote industrial enterprises and to encourage the construction of railways and harbours and the establishment of banking and commercial undertakings. But their success was limited. In the Brazilian census of 1920 it was revealed that of the total capital invested in industry by that year, less than 10 per cent had been invested before 1885. The main reason was probably the insufficiency of the home market. Not only was the population relatively small, but it was widely scattered over a territory of poor communications. In addition, the old colonial plantation economy still left its traces. The population was in the main divided into two: the very rich and the very poor. For reasons of prestige and snobbery in part, but also because of a genuine preference for the better article, the rich insisted on goods of foreign manufacture; the poor couldn't afford any at all.

Several factors then began to influence the situation; first, the large influx of European immigrants towards the end of the empire and the first quarter of a century of the republic. They began to provide that solid basis of a middle class that is the real nucleus of a home market. Second, the coffee boom began to concentrate population, first in the Paraíba valley and later in São Paulo, and so was initiated that increase in population in what has been called here the mountainous area of the south-east, where is still to be found by far the biggest market for consumer goods in Brazil. Third, the beginning of the use of hydro-electric power; the first plant of 52 kw. only was installed in 1883. These and other factors led to a remarkable expansion. It has been noted

Brazil

that of the capital invested in industry by 1920, only 10 per cent had been applied before 1885; between 1885 and 1895 the figure is 20 per cent. Between 1895 and 1905 progress was not so rapid, and only 11 per cent of capital invested by 1920 corresponds to that period; but 31 per cent of the 1920 figure was invested between 1905 and 1914, and 25 per cent between 1914 and 1920. Of great assistance to Brazilian industry was the introduction of the so-called gold tariff under President Campos Salles in 1905. By this tariff a proportion of customs duties had to be paid in gold, and so in effect meant more protection and greater stability for Brazilian industry. This tariff largely accounts for the marked improvement in industrial development which began in 1905 after the relative lull in the previous ten years. The following table compiled from Roberto Simonsen's study gives only approximate figures for it deals with a time when Brazilian statistics were far from complete or accurate. In addition, the sterling figures given cannot be exact; but they give some idea of the early stages of Brazil's industrial expansion.

	1850	*1889*	*1907*	*1920*
No. of industrial establishments	50	636	3,250	13,336
Capital invested	£780,000	£25,000,000	£42,000,000	£115,000,000
No. of workpeople	?	54,169	150,841	275,512
Power consumption in h.p.	?	65,000	109,284	310,424
Value of annual production	?	£30,000,000	£45,000,000	£185,000,000

It is worth noting, too, how the 1920 industrial production was divided into categories: these were as follows (in percentages).

Food	40·2
Textiles	27·6
Clothing and toilet articles	8·2
Chemical and allied products	7·9
Balance	16·1

Among other factors which helped to achieve this expansion were the exploitation of Brazil's poor resources of coal and the gradual development of communications. Brazilian coal began to be used in 1914, and production was stimulated in 1931 by

Emancipation: Political, Economic, and Cultural

compelling all importers of foreign coal to buy national coal equal in quantity to 10 per cent of the coal they imported; they are now required to buy 20 per cent. The rise in production between 1930 and 1938 was considerable (from 376,852 tons to 854,985 tons), but the Second World War provided a further stimulus and by 1945 production was over 2 million tons.

TRANSPORT

The building of the first railway in Brazil was begun in 1853, and by 1860 about 220 kilometres were in operation. Expansion was not rapid, and by the end of the empire in 1889, only 9,500 kilometres of track had been laid. By 1914 this had been increased to 26,000. But progress since then has been even slower; in the thirty-three years between 1914 and 1948, only about 11,500 kilometres have been added. The poor profits to be made on any lines not in the most highly populated area, and the losses suffered by foreign investors have been a deterrent; but even more so, the development of road and air transport, as well as the well-established coastal shipping services, have prevented further railway development. On the other hand, a number of lines have been successfully electrified, and other electrifications are being vigorously pushed forward. The distribution of railways in the various states shows how large is the preponderance of what has been called the mountainous area of the south-east. The figures given are for 1949, in kilometres.

Minas Gerais	8,597
São Paulo	7,590
Rio Grande do Sul	3,661
Rio de Janeiro, including Federal District	2,823
Bahia	2,423
Paraná	1,741
Ceará	1,380
Santa Catarina	1,215
Pernambuco	1,157
Remaining states	5,405
Total	35,992

(SOURCE: *Anuário estatístico do Brasil*, 1950)

There do not appear to be any figures available in the matter of road building, but there has clearly been great activity in the last twenty years. Many roads in rural areas are hardly more than primitive dirt tracks, but in the more populous areas there are

Brazil

magnificent highways; one example is the road from São Paulo to its port of Santos, along which buses now run at the rate of eight or nine an hour. The best way of assessing the increase in motor traffic is to examine the figures for passenger cars, buses, and lorries in 1939 and again ten years later.

	1939	*1949*
Private cars	122,061	192,679
Buses	5,965	21,157
Lorries (all sizes)	74,786	161,340
	202,812	375,176

(SOURCE: Ministry of Foreign Affairs, *Brazil, 1940–1*.)

The rise in the number of motor vehicles on Brazilian roads has been fully maintained since 1949; in 1952 the total number of road vehicles was 544,566.[1]

There is a well-established coastal trade. Indeed, except for air lines, the sea route is the only means of transport between some of the northern cities, and between the north and north-east on the one hand, and the centre and south on the other. Until not long before the war it was not abnormal to travel from Rio de Janeiro to São Paulo by sea through the port of Santos; and many preferred the sea journey from Santos to Paranaguá to the tedious rail journey or uncomfortable road between São Paulo and Curitiba. German attacks and lack of replacements (in spite of the shipbuilding yards now to be found in Rio de Janeiro) reduced Brazilian shipping from 513,000 gross tons in 1940 to 440,000 in 1945. By 1947 it had recovered to 723,000 gross tons. Most of these vessels are small, and in 1947 the total tonnage represented nearly 314 ships. There has been some reduction since 1949 when a peak of 407 vessels with a gross tonnage of 814,810 was reached. The figure for 1951 is 300 vessels with a gross tonnage of 536,647. It is probable that the increased popularity of air travel has reduced the number of passengers using coastal shipping lines.

Air travel has made a very real difference to Brazil. In a country so large and where communications are so difficult, it was bound to have a fairly rapid development. Journeys that not so long ago might well take a month of difficult and arduous travelling can now be accomplished in little more than a few hours. It has meant that all the larger centres are in quick, easy, and fre-

[1] W. Godfrey, *Brazil* (London, H.M.S.O., 1954; Overseas Economic Surveys).

Emancipation: Political, Economic, and Cultural

quent communication with each other, and that there is more movement and traffic in the less important regions. Even the remote territories now receive travellers from all parts of the country. Guaporé, Acre, Rio Branco, and Amapá received respectively 2,720, 2,180, 1,239, and 3,096 air travellers in 1951. Brazilians themselves have taken a leading part in this expansion of the air network, and about 80 per cent of the air traffic of Brazil is in Brazilian hands. The following table gives some idea of the expansion that has taken place.

	1939 Total	*1951* Total	Brazilian lines
Passenger km.	41,504,000	1,492,370,078	1,239,705,289
Ton km. baggage	770,611	23,945,768	18,930,382
Ton km. mail	477,940	2,992,681	1,762,389
Ton km. cargo	438,874	48,691,758	46,311,997

(SOURCE: *Anuário estatístico do Brasil*, 1952)

This rapid survey of Brazilian industrial development and the causes that led to it makes no pretence to being complete. Nor does it attempt to sum up the present economic situation; that will be attempted in Chapter V. But it does show that the industrialization of Brazil is as natural a development as was the industrialization of the United States. It has not been economic nationalism, nor a vain hope of economic self-sufficiency that has led to it. Only for relatively short periods has Brazil adopted a fully protectionist policy. Even the so-called gold tariff was discontinued in 1934, as will be seen later. There have been British financiers and industrialists who have adversely criticized the development, and have expressed the view that Brazil belongs to those areas of the world that can best and most efficiently produce raw materials only. The fact is that Brazil has done no more, and in fact, rather less, than is required for a nation simultaneously improving its standards of living and increasing its population roughly at the rate of a million a year.

FOREIGN INVESTMENTS

Under the general heading of economic emancipation there is one more subject that must be examined before passing on to the consideration of the cultural development of the country; and this is the matter of foreign investments in Brazil. Foreign capital has done a great deal in the development of the country, and

Brazil

loans, mostly negotiated in London, have more than once prevented economic and financial disaster. In their recent book on the economy of Brazil,[1] George Wythe and his assistants produce a table showing Brazil's foreign debt in 1930. Since then, as they point out, there have been no developments except for funding arrangements and readjustments. The table shows the debts incurred by the federal government, the states, and the municipalities (in millions of currency units):

	Pounds	Francs	Dollars	Florins	Total in Pounds
Federal Government	99·8	1,262·7	147·4	—	141·2
States	50·6	227·5	157·5	10·7	86·6
Municipalities	10·7	50·0	68·3	—	25·5
TOTAL	161·1	1,540·2	373·5	10·7	253·3

Although Brazil never wholly defaulted on these loans, it frequently found great difficulty in servicing the very considerable external debt. On several occasions it was necessary to suspend cash remittances and to resort to funding. This can be understood when it is remembered that until recently the value of Brazilian currency in relation to all the currencies in which the loans had been obtained, except for French francs, was constantly falling. In fact, combined with the service on the internal debt, Brazil had to set aside nearly 40 per cent of the budget for the servicing of the national debt in 1930. Clearly this was a situation which could not continue. This explains why there have been various fundings, adjustments, and consolidations, which have substantially reduced the external debt. In view of the devaluation of sterling, no effective comparisons can be made in pounds, and it is best to calculate in dollars. The total figure of Brazil's foreign debt in 1930 (£253,300,000) was equivalent to $1,266,500,000, whereas by the end of 1947 it amounted to no more than approximately $670 million, although in calculating the foreign-debt service a number of obligations to United States special agencies, amounting to just under $140 million must be taken into account. The net result is that the servicing of the whole of Brazil's national debt took up less than 9 per cent of the 1948 budget.

Apart from official federal, state, and municipal loans, there is a good deal of foreign capital invested in Brazil. The 1940 census

[1] *Brazil, an Expanding Economy* (New York, Twentieth Century Fund, 1949), p. 295.

Emancipation: Political, Economic, and Cultural

showed that out of a total capital of 4,543 million cruzeiros of commercial houses, 1,627 million cruzeiros were held by foreigners. The same census showed in regard to industrial undertakings that of a total capital of 7,273 million cruzeiros, 2,985 million cruzeiros were foreign-owned. The 1950 census shows a total capital investment in industry of 52,000 million and when the figures have been analysed a reduced proportion of foreign-held capital will almost certainly be shown. One noteworthy aspect of the position is the fact that whereas British investment in Brazil is steadily declining, American investment as steadily increases. The early example of such enterprises as Coats (cotton thread), and, on a smaller scale, Clarks (shoes), in spite of their success, was not followed by other British manufacturers of consumer goods, but has been followed by the Americans (nylon, rubber tyres, etc.) who were estimated to have nearly $70 million invested in Brazilian manufacturing firms. Britain, on the other hand, has lost a number of holdings in railways and other enterprises, which have been taken over by the Brazilian government and for which compensation has been or is being paid; among these are the São Paulo Railway, the Great Western Railway of Brazil, the Leopoldina Railway and the Bahia South Western Railway. Mr George Wythe estimated the total value of foreign investments in 1949 as $1,500 million, and suggests that the probable distribution as between nationalities is as follows (in million dollars):[1]

British	550–600
United States	450–500
Canadian	200

and the balance divided between the French, Belgians, Portuguese, Dutch, Swiss, and Argentines.

CULTURAL DEVELOPMENT

It is relatively easy to discuss Brazil's political and economic emancipation. There are events to be noted, dates to be recorded, personalities to be discussed, and, on the economic side, there are statistics of production, industrial plants, imports and exports, which almost by themselves tell the story of gradual development with scarcely any need for interpretation and explanation. On the cultural side, the task is far more difficult, and in a brief

[1] *Brazil, an Expanding Economy*, p. 299.

Brazil

study of this nature only a cursory examination can be made if the danger of lapsing into long catalogues of meaningless names is to be avoided.

In Chapter II it was shown that the Portuguese colonists and settlers found no established civilization or culture in Brazil. It cannot therefore be said that there was any indigenous foundation to be fertilized by the culture of Portugal. Not only that, but the early Portuguese settlers were not themselves culturally inclined. There is not in the history of Brazilian letters any equivalent to the half Inca, Garcilaso de la Vega, who was writing the *Comentarios Reales de los Incas* at a time when Cervantes was creating Don Quixote, and at once destroying the Middle Ages and creating a standard of conduct and a mode of thought which the Western world has not yet outlived, and possibly never will. In fact, some students go as far as to say that there was no culture in Brazil until the setting up of the independent empire. Stefan Zweig, considering the culture of Brazil, writes as follows: 'In order properly to appreciate this specific accomplishment, one must not forget that the whole intellectual life of this nation is hardly more than one hundred years old, and that in the preceding three hundred colonial years, every form of cultural development had been systematically suppressed.'[1]

In a sense, what Zweig says is true: in Brazil, papers could not be printed before 1800. Such education as there was in colonial times was entirely in the hands of religious orders, and mainly of the Jesuits, who were expelled in 1760; it is true, too, for many years after the independence that the vast mass of the population remained illiterate. But this is true also of many other countries, and by no means only of the ex-colonial nations; and culture is not exclusively a product of intellectual life. Perhaps the most obvious example of non-intellectual culture is the folk music of Brazil. Even today, the majority of the popular and successful carnival songs originate in the *favelas*, or shanty districts, on the hills of Rio de Janeiro, in much the same way as the calypsos of Trinidad, though they seem to have a greater strength and originality than the West Indian product. However, the fact remains that there was little independent cultural development in Brazil before the nineteenth century; and no one would dispute Zweig's general thesis.

Gilberto Freyre, the Brazilian thinker and sociologist, draws

[1] *Brazil, Land of the Future* (London, Cassell, 1942), p. 155.

Emancipation: Political, Economic, and Cultural

attention to the first authentic example of Brazilian culture. He writes:

For a long time, Brazilian art and literature remained almost inarticulate and passively colonial or sub-European. Aleijadinho, the mulatto sculptor of eighteenth-century colonial churches in the gold-mine region of Brazil, was one of the few artists to appear with a socially significant artistic message and a technique distinguished by creativeness, audacity, and non-European characteristics in a century marked, in Brazil, by academic literature and imitative art.[1]

Freyre goes on to describe the sculpture of the diseased mulatto Aleijadinho as the first Brazilian expression of social revolt. He goes so far as to describe him as 'a sort of mulatto El Greco', and as a forerunner of the Mexican, Diego Rivera, and the Brazilian, Portinari. Many will not be prepared to go as far as Gilberto Freyre, but undoubtedly the religious sculptures and figures of Aleijadinho are of very real merit, and represent a new pheomenon in the story of colonial Brazil.

LITERATURE

In the world of letters, in spite of what Stefan Zweig suggests, there are many names worth recording. Ronald de Carvalho[2] divides the history of Brazilian literature into three periods. First, a formative period when there was an absolute ascendancy of Portuguese thought (1500–1750); second, a period of transformation when the poets of the school of Minas Gerais began to neutralize, though only slightly, the effects of Portuguese influence (1750–1830); and third, a period of greater autonomy during which the romantics and 'naturalists' brought to Brazilian literature new European currents (1830 onwards). This classification alone is enough to emphasize how little there has been until relatively recently of genuine Brazilian literary production. On the other hand, Brazil's slow start has been more than compensated for by the rapidity of her literary development in the second half of the nineteenth century. Nevertheless, Ronald de Carvalho is right when he attributes to the poets of Minas Gerais in the late eighteenth century (about the same time as the development of the sculpture of Aleijadinho) the first signs of Brazilian, as opposed to imitative and neo-European, characteristics. There is need only to recall the historical poem *O Uruguay* (1769) by José Basílio da

[1] *Brazil, an Interpretation* (New York, Knopf, 1945), p. 155.
[2] *Pequena história da literatura brasileira*, 6th ed. (Rio de Janeiro, Briguiet, 1937).

Brazil

Gama (1741–95) to realize that Minas Gerais was perhaps the birthplace of Brazilian literature as we know it today.

From 1830 onwards, the influence of French romanticism on Brazilian poetry was profound. Nevertheless it led to the development of what Samuel Putnam[1] has called 'the greatest poet that Brazil had yet produced', Antônio Gonçalves Dias (1823–64). His *Poesias americanas*, says Putnam, have been seen as 'combining the spirit of the Indian, the Negro, and the Portuguese—the three principal ethnic factors in Brazil'. There is space to mention only one of the many other poets who have achieved distinction in Brazil since Antônio Gonçalves Dias: Antônio de Castro Alves, the 'poet of the slaves'. Castro Alves (1847–71) indulged in great poetic eloquence, even grandiloquence, but he was nevertheless of profound poetic feeling and used his talents to advocate the abolition of slavery. It is worth recording also the names of four modern poets whose influence has been very strong in recent years: Jorge de Lima, Murilo Mendes, Carlos Drummond de Andrade, and Manuel Bandeira.

But it was not in verse alone that the emancipation of Brazilian letters was brought about; in some ways the development of the novel was even stronger. Joaquim Manuel de Macedo (1820–82) is not a writer of great prestige among literary circles. Nevertheless, at least two of his homely tales are widely read by Brazilians down to the present day, *A moreninha* and *O moço loiro*. José Martiniano de Alencar (1829–77) chose characteristically Brazilian and often Indian themes for his novels and perhaps the best known, because it was the basis of the libretto for the opera by Carlos Gomes, is *O Guarany*. However, as Stefan Zweig points out, this is no more than an expression of the European fashion for the 'noble savage', and in a sense imitative of Chateaubriand's *Atala* and similar works. But in the second half of the nineteenth century, three names set the seal on the complete emancipation of the Brazilian novel: Graça Aranha (1868–1931), Machado de Assis (1839–1908), and Euclydes da Cunha (1866–1909). Aranha's *Chanaan*, Machado de Assis's *Dom Casmurro*, and above all da Cunha's *Os sertões*, began Brazil's contribution to Western literature. No longer were Brazilian authors good imitative craftsmen; they were making a positive contribution to Western letters, not in content only, but also, particularly in the case of da Cunha's

---

[1] 'Literature', in Lawrence F. Hill, ed., *Brazil* (Berkeley and Los Angeles, University of California Press, 1947), p. 213.

Emancipation: Political, Economic, and Cultural

Os sertões, in form as well. Today Brazilian novelists are perhaps too much influenced by advanced European thought; the influence of Lawrence, Joyce, Gide, and Freud are particularly noticeable. Nevertheless, the modern writers are producing fine and powerful work; Graciliano Ramos, Lúcio Cardoso, Erico Veríssimo, Jorge Amado, José Lins do Rego are only a few of a talented group producing new novels. Nor is the work of Brazilian thinkers, and in particular of the sociologist, Gilberto Freyre, to be forgotten. Brazil today is no longer an outpost of European letters; it is in fact the leading centre of Portuguese thought and letters. As the Portuguese language is better known, and it surely will be in view of the growing importance of Brazil, and as more of the best works are translated into English and other European languages, Brazil may well come to exert some influence on Western letters.

MUSIC

In music, in spite of the wealth and variety of popular dances and songs, Brazil was slower to achieve emancipation. Carlos Gomes (1836–96) was the only nineteenth-century Brazilian composer to achieve fame outside his own country. A successful beginning at the age of twenty-four with the opera *A Noite do Castello*, performed in Rio de Janeiro in 1861, attracted the attention of the Emperor, who sent him to Italy to study. There, however, Gomes became completely Europeanized, and in spite of the brilliant success of *Il Guarany* (based on the novel *O Guarany* by Alencar), he never justified the high hopes that his youth had inspired. Another opera, *Lo Schiavo*, is said to be superior, but has never been performed outside Brazil. The extent of his dependence on non-Brazilian inspiration may be measured by a cruel comment on *Il Guarany*—Meyerbeer's best opera.

Without doubt it is Heitor Villa-Lobos (born in 1884) who has at last achieved a real Brazilian music of a high order, though strangely enough Brazilian influence has already been felt in Western music in other ways; an example is the *Saudades* of Darius Milhaud. Villa-Lobos has achieved fame not only by the use of original orchestration but by his able use of Brazilian themes and rhythms. It is probably in his various *Chôros* that he has most distinguished himself, but his symphonic poems and some of his symphonies are also widely known, particularly in the United States. He himself conducted the B.B.C. Symphony Orchestra in

Brazil

London in 1948 for the first performance of his Seventh Symphony. Many consider that the greatest of his works are the *Bachianas*, but they are rarely if ever heard in Britain. Other composers of note today are Lorenzo Fernandez, Francisco Mignone, Camargo Guarnieri, and Radamés Gnattali, who was once hailed as a Brazilian Gershwin. It is still too early to pass judgement on the younger composers of Brazil, but it is already clear that the future will bring a great wealth of originality and that Brazil is to make a valuable contribution to Western music.

ARCHITECTURE, SCULPTURE, AND PAINTING

Perhaps the most obvious advance made by Brazil—particularly to the stranger visiting Rio de Janeiro and São Paulo—is in architecture. There is no doubt that the Swiss architect, Le Corbusier, had a great influence on the modern architecture of Brazil, but it is equally certain that the Brazilians have branched off independently and created what amounts to a new school of modern tropical architecture. No one who sees the buildings of the Ministry of Education in Rio de Janeiro and of the Associação Brasileira da Imprensa, or other public buildings and apartment houses throughout the country, can doubt the fact that in this matter of tropical architecture Brazil has not only emancipated itself but, in fact, leads the way. Lúcio Costa and Oscar Niemeyer are perhaps the most famous names among a brilliant group of designers. Nor does Brazil lag behind in the matter of town planning; Belo Horizonte, capital of the State of Minas Gerais, was the first state capital to be planned from its foundations. Its success has led to a similar experiment now being carried out in the state of Goyás, whose capital Goiânia was planned in the same way. A site has been selected in the same state for the eventual building of a federal capital, though it is difficult to see how a transfer from Rio de Janeiro could be achieved without an immense dislocation and a great deal of inconvenience.

In sculpture the tradition of Aleijadinho did not outlive him, and there were no memorable successors. It was not until the growth of so-called modernism that sculptors such as Vítor Brecheret and Celso Antônio began to make their name; today among the leading Brazilian sculptors are to be found Bruno Giorgi, Adriana Janacópoulos, and Figueira. Modern Brazilian sculptors seem to be much influenced by the French.

Emancipation: Political, Economic, and Cultural

In spite of the fact that during the empire painting was perhaps the most popular of the arts, there are no really great figures in Brazilian painting until the present day. It was not until during and after the First World War that experimental tendencies gained the ascendancy and produced several painters of vigour and originality who are not, nevertheless, much known outside Brazil. Cândido Portinari is undoubtedly the leading contemporary painter and his paintings, murals, and engravings are increasingly known in the United States and Europe.

SCIENCE, TECHNOLOGY, AND MEDICINE

In science, mathematics, and technology, it is more difficult to assess the position of Brazil, and no attempt can be made to do more than mention a few outstanding names. Among these must be the mathematician Benjamin Constant, one of the leaders of the revolt against Dom Pedro and first Minister of Education of the republic, who played an important part in the foundation of the republic, and who brought to Brazil the influence of Auguste Comte—an influence which affected many Brazilian mathematicians. To this day there are a number of Brazilians who are attracted by positivism.

Perhaps better known is Santos-Dumont, the pioneer in aviation, who was undoubtedly the first man to fly a rigid lighter-than-air craft (in Paris, 1901), and in 1906 made a flight with a heavier-than-air machine. There is no point in pursuing the argument between the admirers of Santos-Dumont and those of the Wright Brothers as to which can legitimately claim to be the first. The fact remains that Santos-Dumont was a real pioneer of the air, and that his contribution to aeronautics in its early days was of immense value.

Dr Oswaldo Cruz is one of the great names in tropical sanitation. His work, which attracted world-wide attention and led to visits to Brazil of many distinguished foreign experts, is commemorated in the institute that bears his name, but perhaps his greatest monument is the fact that the tropical city of Rio de Janeiro is free from malaria and yellow fever.

Brazilians can claim to have made worth-while contributions to sea navigation, mass radiology, and many other specialized branches of study; they have produced distinguished naturalists and geologists. Today, with the growth and development of uni-

Brazil

versities and the spread of popular education, there is every reason to suppose that Brazil will easily hold her place among the nations of the world.

Enough has been said to show that since Brazil gained her nominal political emancipation in 1822, she has forged ahead, erratically, perhaps, but surely, so that today she is nearer to economic and cultural emancipation than any other tropical ex-colonial area in the world. If this is largely due to the wealth of her soil and other favourable conditions, it is due also to the qualities of the Brazilian people, their tolerance, their good sense, and their undoubted intelligence.

CHAPTER IV

EXAMPLE: COLONIZATION AND FOREIGN POLICY

IN the introduction Brazil is described not only as a land of contrast and experiment and as a country of recent emancipation, but also as an example. In spite of recent progress and many successes, Brazil must be classified at present as one of the less developed and less advanced nations of the world. How then can this little advanced country present an example to any nation?

One instance has already been considered: miscegenation and the relative absence of racial prejudice. In Chapter II it was shown that miscegenation was not a conscious and purposeful policy: nevertheless it has become one. Indeed, it is almost a matter for regret that Brazilians should now be conscious of their almost total lack of racial barriers. Unfortunately, this awareness is inevitable in a world which has only just defeated Nazism. On the credit side is the fact that this awareness of the racial question in Brazil has not led to any reaction against miscegenation, but on the contrary to a consciousness of a serious danger escaped and to a realization among the more distinguished Brazilian thinkers of the contribution to world civilization that this accident of history has made possible.

SELF-COLONIZATION

It is not only in racial matters that there are lessons to be learned from Brazil. There is also the problem of colonization. Brazil is a vast area of which the greater part is under-populated: it presents, therefore, a serious temptation to any over-populated country in search of room for expansion; there can be little speculation on what would have happened to Brazil if Germany had won the Second World War. Brazil's policy in regard to under-populated areas is therefore of world importance. The early period of colonization presents a story no different from that of any other colonial area, except for the fact that it was to a large extent a Brazilian people, rather than a colonizing European

Brazil

immigration, that first opened up the interior. It was the *mamelucos* of mixed blood—the so-called *bandeirantes*—who first opened up the interior. Their record is no better than that of any other colonizing people. In their period of expansion and their spread from São Paulo down to the southern plains and up into Minas Gerais and the São Francisco valley, they paid little heed to the indigenous Indian; the Indian whose blood ran in their veins. On the contrary, one of their aims was to capture Indian slaves. It was at this early stage that the traditional and bitter enmity between civilized man and the savage Indian was established; and this created a problem for the republic at the end of the nineteenth century and the beginning of the twentieth which has not proved easy to solve. In Chapter I it was shown that nearly 90 per cent of the population of Brazil lives in rather less than a third of the area of the country, mostly near the coast, and the rest in the vast interior; but this does not present a complete picture. The thinly populated areas are even more unevenly populated than the rest: enormous zones seem to be able to support only the scantiest population, and that at a very low level indeed. Brazil's task of the incorporation of the Indian into the life of the nation is not numerically as great as that of other Latin American countries, as for example, Peru and Mexico, where between a third and a half of the population is still unable to speak or understand Spanish, let alone read or write it. But geographically Brazil's difficulties are greater; and they are greater, too, in so far as there is little or no homogeneity between the different groups of Indians.

In the interior of Brazil are to be found many different tribes; the remnants of peoples who refused to accept slavery or serfdom in the Spanish and Portuguese settlements in the coastal areas of the continent; peoples who gradually retreated, sometimes across the Andes and sometimes up the great jungle rivers, into the centre of South America—a huge area between the Andes on the west and the Brazilian central plateau on the east, and between the north-west of the Amazon basin and the plains and pampas of Paraguay and the north of Argentina. From the central zone of the continent spring waters that feed the Amazon and the Plate, and in the rainy season it is a matter of chance whether a drop of water will ultimately find its way to the Amazon basin and out into the equatorial Atlantic, or to the basin of the River Plate and out into the South Atlantic. It is an area of floods and jungles, of

Example: Colonization and Foreign Policy

deserts and marshes; an area of wild beasts and snakes and dangerous insects; an area peopled by innumerable tribes.[1] All these tribes are to be found in the state of Mato Grosso, in the southwest of the state of Amazonas, and in the territory of Guaporé. It is an area of about half a million square kilometres—rather bigger than the area of France—and today it is known as Rondônia, because the work of colonization, of exploration and civilization, has been carried out mainly under the guidance and inspiration of one man, General Cândido Mariano Rondon. The task is far from finished, though it is now nearly half a century since Rondon first appeared on the scene.

THE WORK OF GENERAL RONDON

It was at the very end of the nineteenth century that Brazilian official and public attention was first concentrated on the far west. The search for more rubber in the upper reaches of the Amazon, frontier disputes with Bolivia, and the setting up of an abortive rebel republic under a Spanish adventurer, Gálvez, all combined to bring home the need for military help in the establishment of law and order, and the protection of distant frontiers; and, at

[1] In an appendix to *Rondon* (Rio de Janeiro, José Olympio, 1942) by Clovis de Gusmão the following summary of the different tribes and their origins appears:
'From the Andes came the Aruaks; from the Atlantic seaboard the Guês; from the Amazon the Tupís and the Caraibes; from the Chaco offshoots of the Otuquís. In the north live in the valley of the Gi-Paraná, the Parnauats, the Tacuateps, the Urumís, the Urupás and the Jarús; in the valley of the Tapajós, the Apiacás, and the Mundurucús; in the valley of the Xingú, the Auitis, the Camaiuras, the Trumains and the Manitsauás. In the east live in the valley of Tapirapé the people known under that name; in the valley of the Araguaia, the Caaiapós, the Carajás and the Chavantes; to the west in the valley of the Madeira, the Caripunas; in the valley of the Jamarí, the Arikêmes; in the valley of the Candeia, the Ramas-Ramas and the Bocas-Negras; in the valley of the Mamoré, the Pacaas-Novos; in the valley of the São Miguel and its tributaries, the Uomos and the Puros-Boros; and the Ariás and Macuropes in the valley of the Guaporé; in the open land of Pan Cerne are the Guaraias. In the south are to be found in the valley of the Dourados the Caiuás; in the valley of the Nabileque, and in Nabileque and Lalima, the Guaicurús; in the valley of the Miranda, the Terenos. In the central zone live in the basin of the São Lourenço the Borôros, and in the delta of the São Lourenço, as it flows into the Paraguai, the Barbados; between the rivers Ponte de Pedra and Papagaio, the Parecís; between the rivers Juruena and Comemoração, the Nhambiquaras; in the valley of the Pimenta Bueno the Keptriuats; in the valley of the River Verde, a tributary of Paranatinga, the Cajabis; in the upper Paranatinga valley, the Bakairis; as well as dozens of other tribes isolated between the valleys of the Gi-Paraná and the River Roosevelt, who have no contact with civilization' (p. 222).

Brazil

least as important in the days before radio communications were practicable, the building of strategic telegraph lines. It was in this atmosphere that the young ensign, later captain, Rondon, began to work in the army telegraphic service. His home was at Cuiabá, capital of the state of Mato Grosso. In spite of the high proportion of Indians that had been incorporated into the life of the nation by the missionaries and the *bandeirantes* in colonial times, there remained a great deal to be done. Even in the west of the state of São Paulo there were savage Indians in the twentieth century. It will be remembered that when the *bandeirantes* were still at work in the late eighteenth century, a great many were drawn to Minas Gerais as a result of the discovery of gold. But it was not only in Minas Gerais that gold was found; it was discovered also in the state of Mato Grosso. On the banks of the river Guaporé the Portuguese built the city of Vila Bela da Santísima Trinidade. Barges laden with gold went down the Guaporé and so into the Amazon, and ships from Lisbon called at Belém to take to Portugal the gold collected by hardy pioneers and gold prospectors in the upper Guaporé valley. Pombal caused massive forts to be built, for the Spaniards in the south and west were also in search of gold and, according to the treaty of Tordesillas, the land belonged to the Spanish crown. Even, for a short while, Pombal thought of establishing the vice-regal capital of Brazil in the far north, where, though in fact much further from Vila Bela, communications along the Amazon and Guaporé were easier and a good deal faster. But it did not last because the alluvial gold was rapidly exhausted; and within a few years the city of Vila Bela was in full decadence and the soldiers were withdrawn from the forts; if there were no gold to be found, it was inconceivable that any European should want to penetrate or even remain in the area. It was in any case a deserted and ruined city that Rondon found when in 1906 he completed his first important task and established telegraphic communication between Cuiabá and Vila Bela.

In 1907 Rondon was called to the presidential palace in Rio de Janeiro and entrusted with the task of building a vast network of telegraphic communications which was to link Cuiabá with the valleys of some of the main tributaries of the Amazon; the Madeira, the Purús, the Juruá, and the Acre. It was a task that called for iron resolution, great courage, and a strong constitution, not on the part of the leader only, but also on that of his lieutenants, and the soldiers, workers, and experts who took part in the work.

Example: Colonization and Foreign Policy

Major Rondon was now the head of the Commission for Telegraphic and Strategic Lines between Mato Grosso and Amazonas. The story of how he accomplished his task is an epic in itself; whole areas were explored for the first time; great rivers were discovered, and Indian tribes pacified. In spite of the hostility of many Indians, and in spite of the lives lost, Rondon held firmly to his view that the Indians must be won over by kindness and not conquered by force. His success was to have a considerable influence, for as his work became known, he became a national figure and almost a legendary hero.

In the meantime troubles with the Indians were being experienced much closer to the populated areas of the country. The state of São Paulo was searching for more suitable land to extend its coffee plantations; a railway was being built to the north-west of the state. But no progress could be made because of the determined and savage opposition of the Caigang Indians. There were two schools of thought; those who urged the use of force and, if necessary, the extermination of the Indians; and those who insisted on pacification and cited the work of Rondon as an example of what could be done. Dr Ihrering of the São Paulo museum published his views in favour of the use of force and provoked strong protests; among them those of Colonel Rondon. 'The Indians', wrote Rondon, 'whoever they may be, are as susceptible as the most sensitive Westerner to love and kindness, not to mention their intelligence, so often met with from colonial times.'

In 1910 the Minister of Agriculture, Rodolfo Miranda, officially called upon Rondon for advice in the matter. His report led to the establishment of the Service for the Protection of the Indians, under the personal guidance of Rondon himself. Its first task was the pacification of the Caigang Indians. The methods laid down by Rondon were simple, but required patience, tenacity, courage, and restraint. A clearing would be made in the jungle at some meeting place of forest paths used by the Indians. A rectangular plot of between 200 to 300 yards in length and breadth was surrounded by barbed wire; in the centre a log cabin provided shelter for about a dozen men. At night the space between the cabin and the wire was illuminated and a gramophone was played to give the impression of constant vigilance. Presents of knives, mirrors, necklaces, and other objects likely to appeal to the Indians, were left in the forest where they were most likely to find them. Gradually, the Indians were convinced of the peaceful

Brazil

intentions of the little settlement; ultimately they responded by themselves leaving presents or by visiting the settlement unarmed. From that stage onwards, the task was easier; there was no interference with tribal customs and no compulsion of any sort. Simple agricultural tools were offered and their methods of use explained; medical treatment was provided; and it was soon discovered that there was much to be gained by exploiting the Indians' love of music. Not only the Caigangs and Coroados of western São Paulo, but also the Stone Age Nhambiquaras in the far north-west, were successfully pacified. Rondon's theory and methods had been proved and justified, and Brazil's colonizing task had been given a policy and an ideal.

Rondon's contribution to the work is incalculable; his idealism and leadership are the admiration of his countrymen and tribute has been paid to him by Theodore Roosevelt, who undertook a journey of exploration together with Rondon just before the First World War. His visit is commemorated in the name of the River Roosevelt. Apart from the exploration of vast areas, the pacification and incorporation into the life of the nation of innumerable Indian tribes, and the publication of many valuable reports, Rondon is credited with the discovery of fifteen major rivers, the setting up of twenty-five telegraph centres, and the building of nearly 15,000 miles of telegraph lines. Nevertheless, there is still much work to be done with the Indians. As recently as 13 March 1951 there were reports of about 2,000 armed and hostile Indians converging upon a settlement on the Xingú river in the state of Pará.

FORTY-SEVEN YEARS OF PEACE

In this problem of colonization and the pacification of savage Indians it was a policy of peace that gained the upper hand. And this was no accident, for the Brazilian is by nature and tradition characteristically peaceful. The same preference for peace has marked Brazil's foreign relations. Stefan Zweig writes:

> Brazil has no desire to expand, nor any imperialistic tendencies. No neighbour can demand anything from her, and she does not demand anything from her neighbours. Never has the peace of the world been threatened by her politics; and even in an unpredictable time such as ours, one cannot imagine that this basic principle of its national conception, this wish for understanding and goodwill, could ever change—

Example: Colonization and Foreign Policy

because this desire for peace, this humanitarian behaviour, has not been an accidental attitude of a single ruler or leader. It is the natural product of a people's character, the innate tolerance of the Brazilian, which again and again has proved itself in the course of history.[1]

No better confirmation of this assessment is needed than an examination of Brazil's foreign policy.

With most ex-colonial countries, there can be no doubt when their foreign policy begins: for normally a country cannot have a foreign policy before it achieves independence. But Brazil, as in so many things, is the exception to the rule. The accident of history that sent the Prince Regent—later Dom João VI—scuttling across the Atlantic, together with his entire court and apparatus of government, gave to Brazil all the attributes of a sovereign nation fourteen years before, in 1822, Pedro I declared the independence of the country. It is true to say, however, that the conduct of foreign affairs was entirely a royal prerogative. War with Napoleon and the conquest of French Guiana were logical developments of the invasion of Portugal by Napoleon's troops in 1807. In effect, the Regent had been forced to choose between the continental elephant of France and the maritime whale of Britain; and as the whale was in a position to sever Brazil from Portugal, and as Britain in any case had a tradition of friendship with Portugal, it is not surprising that the Regent chose Britain. Equally logical, therefore, was the renewal of the Anglo-Portuguese alliance and the signature of a commercial treaty with Britain in 1810. Undoubtedly this treaty gave Britain many trading benefits which enabled her to maintain an easy lead in the foreign trade of Brazil during the first half of the nineteenth century, but in exchange Brazil was assured of British protection—as indeed was Portugal—against any predatory European Power. The British navy was a cardinal factor in Brazil's foreign policy; indeed the famous Monroe doctrine, declared thirteen years later, would have been meaningless but for British naval power.

In the same year as the treaty with Britain the revolution in Buenos Aires began—one of the first explosions which ended in the collapse of Spanish power in Latin America. The Spaniards in Montevideo called on the Regent for help and by 1817 Montevideo was in Brazilian hands; in 1821 it was formally incorporated into Brazil as the Cisplatine Province. But this campaign was not generally popular in Brazil, and it helped to crystallize opinion

[1] *Brazil, Land of the Future*, p. 12.

Brazil

against the Portuguese dynasty; it was an example of a greater preoccupation with European affairs than with the interests of Brazil. The return of Dom João VI to Portugal in 1821, though logical and expected, was psychologically a confirmation of these fears. The illiberal attitude adopted by the Lisbon Constituent Assembly hastened the final break. It was an example of those misfortunes which have proved ultimately to be fortunate for Brazil. When the Regent Dom Pedro was ordered to return to Portugal, there was a spontaneous reaction which led to the 'Fico' (I remain) pronouncement by Dom Pedro, and ultimately, eight months later on 7 September 1822, to the declaration of independence.

Recognition was granted to the new empire by the United States in 1824; but for the security of Brazil what was most essential was recognition by Britain and by Portugal itself. The foreign policy of the young Emperor was directed mainly to obtaining this recognition, but Canning felt that British recognition could not be given before Portuguese. 'What would our situation be,' he writes, 'if Brazil were acknowledged by us as an independent State without the concurrence of the mother country, and if, after such acknowledgement, Brazil was to make war upon Portugal?'[1] From the British point of view, the position was difficult, for Britain had every reason to want to keep alive the conditions of the treaty of 1810 with both Portugal and Brazil, and the position of mediator was made no easier by French attempts to usurp that position and secure for France similar trade advantages. Canning, seconded by Sir Charles Stuart as special envoy, showed consummate skill in these negotiations. By 1825 the task was accomplished, and Brazil soon afterwards established diplomatic relations with the principal European countries.

Perhaps the most striking confirmation of Stefan Zweig's assessment of Brazil as an essentially peace-loving nation is the fact that since the independence it has been involved in only five wars, one of which was a legacy of Dom João VI's Uruguayan conquest, and the others all against militarist dictators. The first of these arose as a result of the revolt of the so-called Banda Oriental and the proclamation of Juan Antonio Lavalleja and his supporters, by which it became a part of the Argentine Confederation; Buenos

---

[1] F.O. 13/7. Dispatch from George Canning to Henry Chamberlain, H.M. Consul-General in Rio de Janeiro, 12 January 1825. Reproduced in C. K. Webster, ed., *Britain and the Independence of Latin America* (London, Oxford University Press, 1938), p. 251.

Example: Colonization and Foreign Policy

Aires accepted the proclamation and Brazil declared war. The land battle of Ituzaingó was indecisive, and even though a Brazilian naval force finally destroyed the Argentine fleet under Admiral William Brown, no final decision could be reached. Once again it was largely British influence which solved the problem. Mainly through Britain's good offices peace was signed in August 1828, in Rio de Janeiro, and the Banda Oriental became the independent República Oriental del Uruguay. Brazil had lost her Cisplatine Province, but once again misfortune was ultimately a gain; the creation of Uruguay made difficult the constant friction and hostility that would undoubtedly have arisen with Argentina had the two countries had a common frontier at the mouth of the River Plate. This is particularly the case in the light of the separatist Farroupilha revolt in Rio Grande do Sul, which began in 1835 and lasted some ten years.

It was not until well after the majority of Dom Pedro II that Brazil was forced again to go to war. In Argentina the dictator Rosas was beginning to put into effect his expansionist dreams, and the Brazilian statesman Pedro de Araújo Lima, then Viscount Olinda, negotiated alliances with Uruguay and Paraguay, which Rosas intended to unite with Buenos Aires. The Argentine troops which were besieging Montevideo were compelled to capitulate in 1849, and Rosas formally declared war on Brazil. An army of Brazilian, Correntine, and Uruguayan troops led by the Argentine General Urquiza and supported by the Brazilian fleet, completely defeated the army of Rosas and destroyed the power of the dictator. There have never again been armed hostilities between Argentina and Brazil.

Sixteen years later, Brazil was again involved in war against another dictator: this time, the notorious Francisco López of Paraguay. The dispute was a long-standing one on the right of way along the Paraguay river to the Brazilian state of Mato Grosso. The only other means of communication between Rio de Janeiro and the western state was up the Amazon and the Guaporé rivers, the route used a century earlier for the gold discovered then in the upper Guaporé valley. In 1855 Brazilian ships and soldiers went up the Paraná river to settle this vexed question, without any satisfactory result. A later treaty giving Brazil the right to navigate the Paraguay was only barely observed, and the Paraguayans treated the Brazilians with the scantiest courtesy. Matters came to a head in 1864, when López seized a

Brazil

Brazilian vessel and simultaneously invaded Mato Grosso, Rio Grande do Sul, and the Argentine province of Corrientes. Argentina, Brazil, and Uruguay entered into a triple alliance and turned the tables on the dictator. The war was long and costly, for López resisted fanatically and his power in Paraguay was absolute. Nevertheless, in 1870 Brazilian troops settled the issue and the capture and death of López with his few remaining troops brought the war to an end. This was the last of the wars in the River Plate area; the friendly relations that have existed since then have been due in no small measure to the conciliatory attitude of Brazil, which even returned to the Paraguayans the military trophies captured during the war.

For forty-seven years afterwards Brazil remained at peace; the story of its foreign policy during those years is largely one of common-sense empiricism. The period is also marked by a decline in British influence and a corresponding increase in United States influence. In addition, Brazil set an example of peaceful international relations by successfully concluding a series of agreements to settle outstanding frontier disputes with neighbouring countries by negotiation or arbitration. During that period, too, occurred the great influx of German and Italian immigrants, not to mention nearly 200,000 Japanese. Far too little was done to ensure the incorporation of these new elements into the nation.[1] The Germans, in particular, were not easily assimilated and in, for example, the state of Santa Catarina there were sizeable towns where no Portuguese was spoken; even negroes living in the town of Blumenau spoke nothing but German, and that with a Pomeranian accent.

BRAZIL AND THE FIRST WORLD WAR

Nevertheless, the outbreak of the First World War found popular opinion in Brazil wholeheartedly upon the side of the Allies. Less than a month after the outbreak of war, a resolution was approved by the Brazilian Chamber of Deputies condemning the violation of treaties and other contraventions of international law. Although the Brazilian government maintained an official attitude of neutrality for three years, most Brazilians, and among them many of pure German descent, were favourable to Britain and her Allies. Sir Malcolm Robertson, who was British chargé

[1] cf. p. 25 above.

Example: Colonization and Foreign Policy

d'affaires in Rio at the time, has since recounted that the Brazilian Foreign Minister, Senhor Lauro Müller—of wholly German extraction—openly sided with Britain to the point of infringing the laws of neutrality.[1] In 1915 Ruy Barbosa, the eminent jurist, founded and accepted the presidency of the Brazilian League for Aiding the Allies. In April 1917 the sinking of Brazilian ships caused Brazil to sever diplomatic relations with Germany, and in October of the same year, Senate and Chamber of the Brazilian Congress passed a resolution recognizing a state of war with Germany. Brazil's war-time policy followed closely upon the actions of the United States; but if officially it lagged behind, unofficially it often led the way, as when Ruy Barbosa made a speech regretting that the United States had not taken the lead and rallied all the American peoples against the German invasion of Belgium and other violations of international law committed by the Central Powers. Materially, Brazil's contribution to the Allied war effort in the First World War was not very great; it would have been surprising if it had been otherwise; but it did bring Brazil for the first time into world politics. She made some contribution in naval activities and one of her warships helped to patrol the west coast of Africa; after the war, King Albert of the Belgians made a courtesy visit to Brazil, mainly as a gesture of appreciation from the Allied leaders for the Brazilian contribution to the war effort.

RELATIONS WITH THE UNITED STATES

But the war and its aftermath brought about two apparently contradictory changes. One was a change that affected the status of all the leading Latin American nations. It is no exaggeration to say, as Professor David Mitrany has done,[2] that the majority of Latin American nations had begun to look upon the United States with increasing fear and irritation. The Monroe doctrine, which a century earlier had been acclaimed, had become an instrument of domination; the famous Roosevelt corollary of 1904 laid it down that lack of order in any country in the Western Hemisphere 'may force the United States, however reluctantly, in flagrant cases of wrong-doing or impotence, to the exercise of an international police power'.[3] The natural result was a series of

[1] 'Brazil enters the War', *Round Table*, December 1942, p. 50.
[2] *American Interpretations* (London, Contact Publications, 1946), p. 65.
[3] President Theodore Roosevelt, message to Congress, December 1904.

Brazil

United States interventions in Caribbean countries including, in 1905, United States control of Dominican customs; between 1906 and 1909, complete control of Cuba; United States financial supervision in Honduras and Nicaragua; the landing of United States Marines in Nicaragua in 1912, in Haiti in 1915, and in the Dominican Republic in 1916. It is not surprising that Latin American nations grew restive at this policy of 'the big stick' (so called by Theodore Roosevelt). The end of the war did not bring United States intervention to an end, but it gave the countries of Latin America a chance for contact with the rest of the world in the League of Nations. Until then, their only opportunities had been at Pan-American congresses; now many of them joined and supported the League, although the United States did not. This alone gave them a feeling of independence. In all these developments Brazil had played a characteristically moderate role. It was not unmindful of the dangers of United States pretensions, but its statesmen never revealed the open hostility expressed by other Latin American leaders, particularly those of Argentina. It was clear that Brazil deplored the United States attitude but realistically appreciated the need for United States friendship. Nevertheless, Brazil joined the League and was elected to the Council; but its first experience of modern European politics proved to be a sharp disillusionment, and it was not long before Brazilian statesmen lost patience with European political intrigue and Brazil withdrew from the League. However, the war had made possible a gesture against the threat of increasing United States tutelage.

But simultaneously a completely opposite tendency had been at work, and United States influence in trade, finance, public utilities, etc., increased astonishingly during these years. The British cable monopoly was broken, and a United States cable company began operating. In 1913 there were no United States loans to Brazil; by 1928 United States loans amounted to 20 per cent of Brazil's foreign indebtedness. In 1913, of Brazil's imports, 15·7 per cent came from the United States and 32·2 per cent of its exports went to the United States; by 1928 these percentages had increased to 26·6 and 45·4 respectively.[1] In effect, the United States during these years completed the gradual process of ousting Britain from the leading position in Brazilian

[1] Figures quoted by Lawrence F. Hill, *Brazil*, p. 364.

Example: Colonization and Foreign Policy

finance and commerce obtained in 1810 and consolidated by Canning in 1825.

Nevertheless, in 1930, when Getúlio Vargas and the Aliança Liberal revolted against the government of Washington Luiz, Brazil had a sharp reminder of United States power and its now traditional attitude to internal disorder in Latin American countries. In October 1930 President Hoover forbade the export of arms to Brazil except with Government authority. This meant, in effect, United States support for the existing government. It was not until after Argentina, Britain, and France had recognized the new government that the United States followed suit.

Since then, largely as a result of President Franklin D. Roosevelt's 'good neighbour' policy, relations between the United States and Brazil have been increasingly cordial. Perhaps this is partly due to an inevitable rivalry between Argentina and Brazil for leadership in Latin American affairs, and to the frequency with which Argentina and the United States were in opposition, as for example the almost personal enmity between Colonel, now General and President, Perón, and Ambassador Braden, later Assistant Secretary of State. As might be expected, too, whenever suspicions arise of Argentine expansionist ambitions, there is a drawing together of Brazil and Chile, one of the two South American countries with whom Brazil has no common frontier. But there is no doubt that friendship with the United States and hemispheric solidarity are now the keystone of Brazilian foreign policy, just as friendship with Britain was the mainspring of her policy in the early days of independence. Needless to say, this does not mean that there is any change in the traditional Anglo-Brazilian friendship. Recent commercial agreements, a cultural treaty, the wide dissemination of books by British authors, and the exceptional popularity of the B.B.C. in Brazil, are all examples of the continuance of that friendship. But materially, financially, and militarily the United States matters more, and the more liberal attitude of United States foreign policy has made possible good relations that are not based on interest alone.

BRAZIL AND THE SECOND WORLD WAR

The test of these two friendships was to come with the Second World War. During the early part of the war, there were some who feared that Brazil might still be inclining to the enemy. A

Brazil

speech made by President Vargas was interpreted as being pro-Axis. Fears born in 1937 that the new Constitution introduced in that year had totalitarian characteristics were revived. Perhaps *The Times* was not far from the truth when it said in a leading article that the 1937 Constitution and the coup d'état of President Vargas was neither Fascism nor Communism, but *Getulismo*.[1] But there was more to it than that. Brazil had achieved during the first four decades of this century the internal unity and national consciousness indispensable for order and progress; and with the exception of the São Paulo revolution of 1932, whose chief characteristic had been the generosity shown to the Paulistas when it was all over, it had done so with less bloodshed than any other large country—as, for example, the U.S.S.R. and China. The Constitution of 1937, which has been described as 'authoritarian democracy', certainly never meant that Brazil was in favour of unprovoked aggression and savage total war. There existed, too, the bogey of the so-called fifth column; the fact is that from this point of view the danger from the German, Italian, and Japanese colonies in Brazil was even less than had been the danger from the Germans in the First World War. In June 1941 President Vargas distinguished between the mass of law-abiding citizens of European descent, which, he said, 'did not preoccupy him', and 'the foreign agents who tried to carry out their disintegrating activities in every country'. In the matter of dealing with those foreign agents, the Brazilian authorities were diligent and effective. Nevertheless, at the beginning of the war Brazil adhered to its traditional policy of peace; its attitude was one of strict neutrality, even though many individuals and organs of the press did not scruple to make clear their sympathy for France and for Britain. It was not until the Rio Conference of the Pan-American Congress that, by supporting the anti-Axis resolutions, Brazil first gave official expression to her sympathy for and solidarity with the Allied cause. Brazil was not blind to its own position; it knew the threat that Vichy-controlled Dakar might represent, and when Dakar fell and Laval returned to office, it was realized that the war had been brought appreciably nearer Brazilian shores. Nor did Brazil fail to appreciate the danger to its shipping, which, if the Battle of the Atlantic were to spread to the south-west, might clearly threaten what, in some cases, provides the only practical

[1] 'Brazil Enters the War', *Round Table*, December 1942, pp. 50-1.

Example: Colonization and Foreign Policy

means of communication, except for air travel, between one important centre and another. Ultimately, it was the sinking of its merchant ships which was the immediate cause of Brazil's entry into the war. The indignation of the people and the press was intensified as the news came through of the loss of ship after ship. Any lingering doubt that the loss of these ships was the logical price of Brazil's uncompromising attitude at the Rio Conference was finally dispelled when it was learned that the Chilean ship *Toltén* had been sunk, in spite of the fact that Chile had not then complied with the recommendation of the Rio Conference that all American nations should sever diplomatic relations with the Axis powers. But Brazil's history proves that her traditional policy of peace is no empty boast, and when the country finally came into the war, on 23 August 1942, its statesmen were anxious to show that its entry implied no change in that policy. The Brazilian Foreign Minister, Senhor Oswaldo Aranha, made a speech emphasizing that Brazil's whole tradition did not permit it to take part in war-like activities except in self-defence. 'That is why,' he added, 'there is no governmental decree declaring war, but merely a law declaring a state of war brought to Brazil's territorial waters by German aggression.'

Brazil's contribution to the Second World War was much more impressive than its contribution to the First. Its strategic position was of incalculable importance. Its air bases were extended and modernized, and placed at the disposal of the United States military authorities; its air force collaborated with the United States in the hunting down of German submarines; its destroyers and corvettes helped in the patrolling of the Atlantic and the protection of convoys; its immense resources of strategic raw materials became available to the Allied nations. Brazil also collaborated with the Allies and supported diplomatic moves in Lisbon, for example, in attempts to put an end to Portuguese supplies of wolfram to Germany.[1] Finally, a Brazilian expeditionary force of more than 20,000 men came to Europe and fought with distinction in the Italian campaign. The United States and Brazil are the only two non-European countries, except for the British dominions, whose troops have fought in Europe since the Moors were chased out of Spain. Brazil emerged from the war with a

[1] Cordell Hull, *Memoirs of Cordell Hull* (London, Hodder & Stoughton, 1948), ii. 423.

Brazil

greatly increased prestige; it was still not a first-class Power, but it was clearly and still remains, a Power to be reckoned with, and a Power in the ascendant.

This increased prestige was reflected in the United Nations when in 1947 Oswaldo Aranha was elected president of the second session of the General Assembly. It has become clear that Brazil has an increasing part to play in world affairs.

CHAPTER V

THE SCENE TODAY: POLITICAL, ECONOMIC, AND SOCIAL

THE FIRST VARGAS REGIME

IN tracing the political development of Brazil, the successful revolution of Getúlio Dornelles Vargas was described in Chapter III. The fact that Vargas, as a result of fairly conducted elections in October 1950, again became president of the republic on 31 January 1951, makes any consideration of his profound influence on the Brazilian scene a matter of today rather than of yesterday; of current events rather than of historical background. Getúlio Vargas had fought the election of 1930 from a reformist platform; he came to sweep out corruption and to break the hold of the old-time politician; it was his intention to free the country from the domination of the old landowning oligarchy in alliance with the rising industrialists. And he lost no time in putting these intentions into practice. In the states, governors were ruthlessly replaced by federal *interventores*, and elected but corrupt officials were replaced by appointed ones. The reaction of the old political bosses was almost immediate; with them were many Paulistas who had looked forward to benefits when Júlio Prestes took office, and some who were upholding separatist tendencies, as well as some state politicians, such as Vargas's erstwhile supporter, Dr Borges de Medeiros, who genuinely feared that the new centralizing tendency would destroy the highly prized autonomy of the states. Gradually, the number of the disaffected increased as Vargas delayed the return to constitutional government; some of his own ministers published critical articles in the press. Finally, in July 1932, the São Paulo revolt broke out.[1]

But Vargas was resolute in opposition. Federal forces under the command of General Góes Monteiro halted the rebel army advancing on Rio de Janeiro under General Bertholdo Klinger. By the end of September General Klinger asked for an armistice; a large part of his army was won over by the Federals and he was eventually compelled to surrender.

[1] cf. p. 47 above.

Brazil

In the meantime, Vargas did not delay his programme of reform. It had always been his view that democracy could not work without a much wider foundation of education; to what extent this was lip-service to democracy it is impossible to say, but the Ministry of Education and Health was in fact drastically reformed. In addition, a new and much-needed Ministry of Labour was set up. Electoral reform was clearly also necessary, but Vargas had learned the lesson of the São Paulo revolt; he already knew when to temporize. He agreed to an election for a Constituent Assembly which was to work out a new Constitution and elect a president of the republic. The election was held in May 1933, and in July 1934 the Constituent Assembly adopted a new Constitution under which Vargas was elected first president by the Assembly. The new Constitution suffered from the defects of compromise; a compromise between those who wished to preserve or even increase the autonomy of the states and those who wished to strengthen the central federal authority. Vargas made no secret of his dissatisfaction with it.

It was not to be expected that while these events were taking place, Brazil would escape the influence of totalitarian ideas. The period was marked by the emergence of a Communist party, under the leadership of Luis Carlos Prestes, and a Fascist party, the Integralistas, under the leadership of Plínio Salgado. In November 1934 Communist uprisings broke out in several widely scattered centres and were supported by several infantry regiments and by a number of air cadets in Rio de Janeiro. The revolt was suppressed by General Eurico Gaspar Dutra, commander of the government forces, and by the Colonel of the air force, Eduardo Gomes; Prestes went into exile, the Communists went underground, and two men of whom more was to be heard had come into prominence: Dutra and Gomes.

Under all of Brazil's Constitutions up to 1945 the presidential term was for four years; the 1934 Constitution was no exception and the Constituent Assembly had elected Vargas to the presidency on that basis. Accordingly, in 1937 the presidential succession once again became a live issue. There were three possible candidates: the official candidate who was endorsed by Vargas, José Américo; the candidate of the old gang supported by the Paulistas and by Flores da Cunha, governor of Rio Grande do Sul; and the Integralista leader, Plínio Salgado. For a time it was thought that Vargas would stand again and the Integralistas,

The Scene Today: Political, Economic, and Social

backed by the German and Italian press did everything in their power to persuade Vargas to stand as their candidate; it was not until he refused that the candidacy of Plínio Salgado was announced. Meanwhile it became known that Flores da Cunha was preparing for a revolution in the south. Vargas took prompt action and reinforced the federal garrison in Rio Grande do Sul. Flores da Cunha fled to Uruguay and as a result the Paulista candidate, Armando Salles, found himself unable to maintain his candidacy. The official candidate, José Américo, proved to be of insufficient calibre; his speeches and declarations were so contradictory and absurd that his chances were destroyed by sheer ridicule. It seemed certain that Plínio Salgado, the *führer* of the Integralistas, would be elected.

But Vargas had no intention of thus letting power slip from his fingers. Instead, he organized a coup d'état, declared a state of emergency, dispensed with the national legislative body, decreed a new Constitution, and once again increased federal authority at the expense of the powers of the states. Even though Vargas had refused to stand as the Integralista candidate, it looked as if he had accepted totalitarianism; *caudilhismo*, the Brazilian version of the traditional Iberian *personalismo*, appeared to have wedded itself to Fascism. A few far-sighted students, as for example the leader writer in *The Times* quoted in the previous chapter, knew better. *Getulismo* might well be dictatorship, but it certainly was not Fascism. Nevertheless, it could not be denied that the popular will had been forestalled and given no chance of expression; democracy had been denied. Here again, however, Brazil's apparent misfortune proved to be of benefit in the end; for a Fascist Brazil, under an Integralista president during the war might well have been a major disaster, not only to the Allied cause, but also to Brazil itself. At the time, however, the Axis Powers welcomed the development and looked to Vargas as a natural ally in their struggle against the democratic Powers.

Their triumph was short-lived. One of the president's first acts after his successful coup d'état was to dissolve all political parties, in particular the Fascist Integralista party. It was this act which led to an armed assault on the Guanabara Palace on 11 May 1938, and to an attempt on the president's life which was frustrated only by the arrival of government troops led by the Minister of War, General Dutra. It has been said that this was one of those blunders that Germany has so often made in its handling of

Brazil

foreign affairs, and that the attempt had the backing of the Wilhelmstrasse. Certain it is that the German ambassador was shortly afterwards handed his passport. However, many Brazilians do not believe this, and hold rather that the return to Germany of the German ambassador was due to a dispute with Oswaldo Aranha, then Brazilian Minister for Foreign Affairs.

Oswaldo Aranha exercised great influence throughout the Vargas regime. Though he seems never to have enjoyed mass popularity in Brazil, and though he did not appear in the cabinet after the 1950 elections, he is now (December 1953) Minister of Finance. He first comes into prominence as the organizer of the Getúlio Vargas revolution of 1930. He was appointed Minister of Justice and Internal Affairs, and as such played a leading part in the internal politics of the beginning of the Vargas regime. At the beginning of 1935 he was sent to take over the Brazilian Embassy in Washington and proved himself to be a first-class diplomat. In spite of rumours and newspaper reports of the pro-Axis leanings of President Vargas, the United States government seemed to maintain the most cordial relations with the Brazilian government; that this was largely the result of the work of Oswaldo Aranha there can be no doubt. But his mission to Washington had a double effect: for he conceived for President Roosevelt a profound admiration, and this must explain in part the rapidity with which Brazil granted the United States air bases, the right to fly military planes over Brazil, and to station military personnel on its soil, shortly after Pearl Harbour. Oswaldo Aranha, too, played a leading part in the anti-Axis resolutions approved at the Rio Conference and, as noted in the previous chapter, was elected president of the General Assembly of the United Nations in 1947; he had been relieved of his post as Minister for Foreign Affairs late in 1944.

The war provided Getúlio Vargas with an admirable excuse to remain in office; in any case, the 1937 Constitution did not specifically determine his term of office. He did, however, promise that elections would be held as soon as the state of the war allowed. The war in Europe came to an end with Getúlio Vargas still in office. There is little doubt that he himself was popular with the masses; but it is equally certain that his government was not. The fact is that it was difficult to be a dictator, to have a completely controlled press, and to maintain such methods of infringing civic

The Scene Today: Political, Economic, and Social

rights as the Tribunal de Segurança, and, at the same time, be the head of a state that had just fought a war in defence of democratic liberties. Meanwhile his popularity with the muzzled press, the business community, and for that matter, with the army, was at a low ebb. Perhaps the last straw was the Pan-American declaration about the freedom of the press at Mexico City. Relying on this, a number of Brazilian newspapermen agreed among themselves simultaneously to disregard the censorship and assert their freedom to criticize the government without restraint. The *Correio da Manhã* of Rio de Janeiro led the way, and the others soon followed. Moderation of expression has never been a Brazilian characteristic and the result was astonishing. To read the Brazilian press would have convinced his most stalwart champion that Vargas had been the least efficient, and was at the time the most unpopular of presidents.

It may be that Vargas was a victim of his own previous refusal to allow freedom to the press: some who were fairly close to him at the time hold that he was genuinely hurt by the cold douche of criticism to which he was subjected. The fact remains that whereas he had previously resisted the counsel of his advisers that he should return to constitutional government, hold elections, and himself retire into private life, he now announced his intention of resigning before the end of 1945 and fixed 2 December as the date for the presidential elections, when he would not be a candidate. However, not only did Vargas have a very real popularity among the masses, but also a fanatical following among a relatively small group of politicians. The result was a series of manifestations in favour of the president's retention of office. Crowds gathered in Rio de Janeiro chanting their slogan 'Queremos Getúlio' (We want Getúlio), and the group became known as the Queremistas. These manifestations alarmed the army which was determined on a change of president; there were in any case many high-ranking officers who did not believe the president's declarations and expected some new manoeuvre on the lines of the 1937 coup d'état. These suspicions were strengthened when Vargas dismissed the chief of police in the Federal District, and appointed in his place his own brother. Accordingly, on 29 October 1945, army units occupied strategic places in Rio de Janeiro, and a group of officers advised the president to resign. This time he yielded and the long Vargas regime came to an end when, constitutionally,

Brazil

Chief Justice José Linhares of the Supreme Court took over the presidency until the elections could be held.

It is not easy to make an assessment of the effects of the Vargas regime. There are a great many things to be placed on the debit side, starting with the unquestioned fact that it was not democratic. But equally there is much to his credit: perhaps the most outstanding contribution was the very considerable programme of social and labour welfare legislation which has largely prevented the ruthless exploitation of industrial workers which marked the industrialization of most other nations. These reforms were possible without serious dislocation at the beginning of the Vargas term of office because industry then represented a much smaller proportion of the national economy than it does now; in addition, the industrialists were not at that stage sufficiently powerful to offer serious opposition. On the other hand, he did not succeed in bringing to an end peculation and corruption among state officials; the huge state insurance funds set up in connexion with the welfare legislation could and should have been held by the government as an anti-inflationary measure: instead they were used for unjustifiable and highly speculative private loans and so accentuated the inflation and the soaring cost of living. The Vargas regime was responsible also for many public works of lasting benefit. Harvey Walker sums them up as follows:

> Strides were taken in the development of reclamation projects in the semi-arid area of the north-east. The Baixada Fluminense, a vast swampland in the state of Rio de Janeiro—many times larger than the Pontine Marshes . . . was drained and placed under cultivation. Advances were made in the realization of the ten-year plan for the construction of highways and railways to link the scattered centres of population in the vast, sprawling country. Experiment stations and agricultural extension services were developed to encourage diversification of agriculture.[1]

Among other developments have been, first, a substantial improvement in education, achieved as a result of strengthening federal authority at the expense of the states, and resulting in conditions much more favourable to democracy; second, a reorganization of the machinery of government by creating a central body responsible directly to the president, known as the Departamento Administrativo do Serviço Público, which combines some

[1] 'The Vargas Regime', in Hill, ed., *Brazil*, p. 116.

The Scene Today: Political, Economic, and Social
functions analogous to those of the British Treasury with those of the office of the Lord President of the Council,[1] and aids the president in matters of interdepartmental co-operation, civil service personnel, purchasing, budgetary, and other matters. This measure was combined with a much stricter competitive selection of senior civil servants. In the third place there has been a great improvement in medical services, and with the aid of the Rockefeller Foundation, yellow fever and typhoid have been brought under control and the incidence of malaria, venereal diseases, and tuberculosis has been greatly reduced. Finally, as a result of all these measures, conditions favourable to many other advances have been created, such as the development of industry, the establishment of air lines, the building of homes, and the creation of a heavy chemical industry.

But, on the debit side must be remembered the Tribunal de Segurança, which made possible imprisonment and exile without adequate trial; the muzzling of the press; the use of the radio for official government propaganda; and the dissolution of all political parties. It was this state of affairs—which had lasted some fifteen years—that made some aspects of the 1945 election wholly unpredictable in that few political names were widely known.

THE 1945 ELECTIONS

Political parties were hastily organized on the announcement of presidential elections, and four candidates appeared. The official candidate was General Eurico Gaspar Dutra (who became prominent at the quelling of the Communist insurrection of 1934), supported by the Partido Social Democrático, which, in spite of its name, represents in the main conservative interests. Dutra's main rival was Air Brigadier Eduardo Gomes (who had tackled the Communist revolt among the air cadets in 1934), supported by the União Democrática Nacional—a slightly more liberal party. The third candidate was Yedo Fiuza, who, though not himself a Communist, accepted Communist support; and there was a fourth candidate, Telles, who had little following. The newly formed Partido Trabalhista Brasileiro—led by Vargas—supported Dutra. The election was fairly held, and out of an electorate of a little more than 7 million, nearly 6 million cast

[1] October 1952.

Brazil

their votes. The result, a complete victory for Dutra, was as follows:

Dutra (Partido Social Democrático, supported by the Partido Trabalhista Brasileiro)	3,251,507
Gomes (União Democrática Nacional)	2,039,341
Fiuza (Communist supported)	569,818
Telles	10,001

In the elections to Congress, the distribution among the parties of senators and deputies was as follows:

Party	Senators	Deputies
P.S.D.	26	151
U.D.N.	10	77
P.T.B.	2	22
Communists	1	14
Others	3	22

But these figures do not accurately reveal the relative strength of the parties: for the candidates were hastily chosen and hardly known to the mass of the electors. Broadcasters, whose names were familiar to the public, obtained many votes simply on the strength of being better known to the electors. Significant, however, was the strength of the newly-formed Partido Trabalhista Brasileiro.

POLITICAL DEVELOPMENTS FROM 1945 TO THE 1950 ELECTIONS

It is perhaps an indication of the strength of the personality of Vargas, that the most important and interesting aspect of the Brazilian political scene has been speculation about his future. After the first flush of victory, when the Dutra administration found that they could do little more than slow down the pace of the increase in cost of living, it became increasingly clear that Vargas could count upon a large proportion of voters. It is undoubtedly still true of Brazil that leaders and personalities count for more than party programmes. This was underlined by the political manoeuvring that went on during the last three years of Dutra's presidential term; the two main parties—the Partido Social Democrático and the União Democrática Nacional—were joined by the Partido Republicano, and as long ago as July 1949 it was announced[1] that these major parties had agreed to put forward a joint presidential candidate at the next elections. But only a day later an analysis was published[2] in the press showing that only 109 of the congressmen who had won the previous

[1] Broadcast by Radio Tupí, Rio de Janeiro, 18 July 1949.
[2] *Diario da Noite* (Rio de Janeiro), 19 July 1949.

The Scene Today: Political, Economic, and Social

election on a P.S.D. ticket continued to support Dutra; fifty-eight were more or less open supporters of Vargas. The more astute politicians showed no great faith in the agreement between the big three. That there was such an agreement is certain; but what is equally certain is that no agreement was ever reached as to who the candidate should be. At about the same time it became clear that Dr Adhemar de Barros, a forceful politician, who founded the Partido Social Progressista and was elected governor of São Paulo in January 1947, himself harboured presidential ambitions; nevertheless, the future was foreshadowed when rumours were reported of an alliance between the Partido Trabalhista Brasileiro (Getúlio Vargas) and the Partido Social Progressista (Adhemar de Barros).[1] This was a serious challenge and the P.S.D. and the U.D.N. leaders redoubled their efforts to reach agreement; for many the possibility of a return to office of Vargas was to be avoided at all costs, and not a few were afraid that the P.T.B. was unduly influenced by the Communists; it seems fairly certain that at one time the Communists considered giving their support to Vargas. The Catholic Church was alarmed and in August 1949 the Meridional news agency published an interview with the Archbishop of Pôrto Alegre in which the Archbishop accused the P.T.B. of Marxist tendencies and of a quasi-Communist programme. In the meantime, the peculiar interplay between party affiliations, state loyalties, and conflicting personalities, proved to be too great an obstacle for the large parties to surmount. On 25 October the U.D.N. announced that no understanding was possible between the big three. Perhaps in the hopes of stimulating a renewal of the discussions, new rumours were put about in January 1950 of an agreement between Vargas and Luis Carlos Prestes, the leader of the Communists. But the position of the Communists was such as to reduce their influence to a minimum; the breaking off of diplomatic relations with Russia and the outlawing of the Communist party seemed at first to be mistaken tactics; in fact, however, the failure of peace campaigns in Brazil, the decline in the sale of extreme left-wing papers, and the gradual realization among many intellectuals that Russia was indulging in power politics, made it more of a liability than an asset to have Communist associations or Communist support. In any case the attempt to form a coalition against Vargas failed. First, Air Brigadier Eduardo Gomes was adopted candidate by U.D.N.,

[1] Broadcast by Radio Nacional, Rio de Janeiro, 16 July 1949.

Brazil

then Getúlio Vargas by P.T.B., and in May 1950 P.S.D. announced their selection of Cristiano Machado as their candidate. Machado is from Minas Gerais, was a federal deputy for Belo Horizonte, and a bank director; but he was not a national figure as Vargas and Gomes undoubtedly are. A fourth candidate was later put forward by the Partido Socialista Brasileiro. In the few months that remained there was feverish work going on. Party alliances were formed, but not so much on a national scale as in each individual state. The final line-up seemed to show that the P.S.D. candidate had every advantage, but the results revealed, not only the enormous popularity of Getúlio Vargas, but also how much more astute he had been than his rivals in making local political alliances. It is interesting to see too how the candidates for the vice-presidency fared; of these there were five, one of whom, Vitorino Freire, stood alone supported by the Partido Social Trabalhista; this fact undoubtedly reduced the lead of the victor; but the fact that the voting for the vice-presidency—among the three leaders—was so much closer than the voting for the presidency is a measure of the effect of the towering personality of Getúlio Vargas.

The results were as follows:

Getúlio Dornelles Vargas	3,829,560
(Partido Trabalhista Brasileiro)	
(Partido Social Progressista)	
Brigadeiro Eduardo Gomes	2,288,105
(União Democrática Nacional)	
(Partido de Representação Popular)	
(Partido Libertador)	
Cristiano Monteiro Machado	1,653,521
(Partido Social Democrático)	
(Partido Trabalhista Nacional)	
(Partido Republicano)	
(Partido Social Trabalhista)	
(Partido Orientador Trabalhista)	
(Partido de Representação Trabalhista)	
João Mangabeira	9,465
(Partido Socialista Brasileiro)	

Results of voting for the vice-presidency were as follows:

The Scene Today: Political, Economic, and Social

Café Filho (P.T.B., P.S.P.)	2,506,955
Odilon Braga (U.D.N., P.R.P., P.L.)	2,291,072
Altino Arantes (P.S.D., P.T.N., P.R., P.O.T., P.R.T.)	1,642,363
Vitorino Freire (P.S.T.)	405,320
Alípio Corrêa Neto (P.S.B.)	10,800

The final result showed that although the progress made by the government parties (P.T.B. and P.S.P.) was considerable, it did not coincide with the presidential voting figures and in both chambers the P.S.D. and U.D.N. parties are still the best represented:

	Senate	Chamber
P.T.B.	7	57
P.S.P.	5	27
P.S.D.	29	106
U.D.N.	14	79
Others	8	35
	63	304

Some form of coalition was necessary and it was known that a substantial proportion of P.S.D. men would collaborate with the president. At the beginning of his administration the cabinet contained four P.S.D. men, one U.D.N., two P.S.P., two P.T.B., and four non-party men.

It is interesting to note that Adhemar de Barros, the leader of P.S.P., does not appear. There are rumours that there had been some disagreement between him and the President; that Adhemar de Barros was to have been given the prefecture of Rio de Janeiro, and that the administration of the Federal District was to have been made independent of the Federal government. In the meantime, however, it is clear that suggestions that the army would not allow Getúlio Vargas to assume office, or that attempts would be made to keep him out on the grounds that he did not secure an absolute majority, had little basis in fact. It is to be hoped that he continues to receive enough support to enable him to govern efficiently; he might otherwise be tempted to adopt dictatorial methods, as in his previous period of office.

Brazil

RELIGION

Little has been said about religion, but as the Church undoubtedly attempted to influence the election, it is perhaps best to consider the religious aspect of Brazil before turning from politics to the present-day economics of the country. As might be expected, the people are predominantly Roman Catholic. Listening to the conversation of upper and middle-class intellectuals, it would be easy to suppose that there is in Brazil a great deal of agnosticism, and, in a religious sense, free thought. In fact, however, the vast majority consider themselves to be Catholic, however superficially they may observe the ordinances of the Church, and however much they may ignore its voice in political affairs. The figures given for the 1940 census are as follows:

Catholic	39,177,880
Protestant	1,074,857
'Espíritas'	463,400
Buddhists	123,353
Jews	55,666
Orthodox	37,953
Mohammedan	3,053
Shintoists	2,358
Positivists	1,099
Other religions, none, or undeclared	296,969

There is no reason to suppose that the 1950 census, when the detailed analysis is available, will reveal any difference in this distribution. Undoubtedly the Church has always had great influence, and, for example, it must be thought doubtful whether the Emperor Dom Pedro II would have fallen so easily had he been as intolerant as the Church would have wished him to be in the matter of freemasonry. On the other hand, the Brazilian would seem to have a clear if undefined idea of the proper sphere of action for the Church. During the presidential campaign in September 1950, the Catholic Electoral League published a list of candidates that could be supported by Catholics; omitted from the list, and widely attacked in Sunday sermons,[1] was Senhor João Café Filho, who was nevertheless elected vice-president—though with a much smaller majority than his principal. But this

---

[1] *Diario Carioca* (Rio de Janeiro), 25 September 1950, and *O Globo* (Rio de Janeiro), 28 September 1950.

The Scene Today: Political, Economic, and Social
does not mean that the Church does not exercise greater influence in other matters; it is said that during President Dutra's early years of office, his wife provided a useful channel for the views of the Church to make themselves felt; one example that has been quoted is the closing of the gaming casino in the luxury Quitandinha Hotel on the road from Rio de Janeiro to the mountain resort of Petrópolis. The Catholic Church is firmly rooted in the traditions and way of life of the Brazilian people. It is hardly necessary to add that it is an important factor in the struggle against Communism.

THE DUTRA ADMINISTRATION

It is too early to try to assess the achievements of the Dutra administration; perhaps its greatest contribution was that it made possible a return to constitutional government and to party political activities. Certainly the 1950 election was fought out with a greater knowledge of the facts and of the candidates among the electorate than the 1945 election, even though, as has been seen before, political programmes still mean less than the personalities of party leaders. Nevertheless, the Dutra government preserved order, and showed that Brazil could be governed, at least as efficiently as ever before, without dictatorship, and without a censorship of press and radio; that in itself was no mean achievement. But when ex-President Dutra reviewed the results of his administration in a speech made on 10 November 1950, it was to economic matters—to agriculture, industry, and transport—that he gave most importance. He listed the construction of 1,300 metres of new docks at Rio de Janeiro; the electrification of the Serra do Mar sector of Central Railway of Brazil, and of the Rio and São Paulo suburban lines, as well as work in progress on the Santos Jundiái, the Leste Brasileiro, and the Viação Paraná Santa Catarina; the work done on some of the main highways, such as the Rio–São Paulo, the Curitiba–Lages and the Rio–Bahia roads; the development of navigation on the São Francisco River, and the progress made with the hydro-electric plant at the Paulo Afonso falls; the fact that the foundations had been laid for Brazil ultimately to become self-sufficient in the matter of wheat; and the reduction of the foreign debt from cr. $10,013,599,663 on 31 December 1945, to cr. $5,620,042,153 on 30 October 1950. On the face of it, this is not a bad record. But

Brazil

President Vargas has not scrupled to announce that his government has inherited a critical economic situation, and his first Minister of Finance pointed out that the note circulation had risen in one year by nearly cr. $7 million; be blames the Dutra administration for the inflation which has so seriously raised the cost of living that Rio de Janeiro can be described as the most expensive capital in the world. Undoubtedly the cost of living increased sharply in the last year of the Dutra administration, but only in relation to the earlier period of his government. During the war years the inflation was at least as great. The table below shows how the situation developed up to 1948.[1]

	Cost of Living		Wholesale Prices	
1939	100		100	
1940	105		107	
1944	191		240	
1945	232		265	
1946	276	100*	298	100*
1947	329	119	371	124
1948	364	132	423	142

* If the 1946 figure is taken as the basis, it can be seen that the increase in 1946–8 is at a lower rate than during the war.

On the other hand it must be borne in mind that a considerable proportion of this inflation is due to the rise in world prices. Nor would it be just to omit the defence of the Minister of Finance in the Dutra government who announced on 6 October 1950 that in August 1950 the note circulation amounted to cr. $27,174 million, and added the following explanation: that whereas in 1944 the note circulation stood at cr. $14,500 million and the national income at cr. $65,000 million in 1949 the note circulation had increased to less than double at cr. $24,000 million and the national income had more than doubled at cr. $150,000 million; an interesting comment, but not in fact a satisfactory explanation of the continued inflation. It is in any case doubtful whether the national income figures can be accepted. What is already clear is that the new Vargas administration has not been able to halt the rise in the cost of living. In spite of the increase in industrial investment, far too much capital is being used to obtain quick profits, particularly in land speculation.

[1] Joint Brazil-United States Technical Commission, *Report* (U.S. Department of State, pub. 3487, Washington, 1949), p. 40.

The Scene Today: Political, Economic, and Social

ECONOMIC POSITION TODAY

But it is not by an examination of the achievements of the Dutra administration that the best survey is obtained of the economic position of Brazil. For in these matters it is not so much the present position as the direction of any change and its relative speed that can give a reasonably reliable guide to the future. If the Brazilian government succeed in doing anything on the lines of the SALTE plan, even though the plan as such has been abandoned, then the fact that it was conceived during ex-President Dutra's term of office may well make it a memorable one; but the fate of the SALTE plan is linked to the future and will therefore be dealt with in the last chapter. This chapter, about the scene today, must first briefly examine the following four tables, based on 1951 returns:[1]

A. Exports from Brazil, classified under products and showing values in cr. $1,000, percentages of total for 1951, and percentages for 1925, 1939, and 1946.
B. Imports to Brazil, classified under types and showing values in cr. $1,000, and percentages of total for 1951 and percentages for 1925, 1939, and 1946.
C. Exports from Brazil classified under country of destination and showing values in cr. $1,000 and percentages of total for 1951, and percentages for 1925, 1939, and 1946.
D. Imports to Brazil classified under country of origin and showing values in cr. $1,000 and percentages of total for 1951 and percentages for 1925, 1939, and 1946.

Table A shows how in 1925 nearly three-quarters of Brazil's exports were coffee, and how cotton, cacao, and timber had been allowed to sink to almost negligible proportions; it shows too that vegetable oils, oleaginous products, vegetable wax, and fruit had hardly been developed at all. The year 1939 saw a considerable improvement; coffee was still an easy first, but Brazil could no longer be described as having a one-product economy; new products were appearing that more than counterbalanced the virtual disappearance of rubber. The war produced a serious dislocation; the European market for many products—in particular the German market for coffee—disappeared, but by 1946 a more normal development was becoming apparent. The real novelty was manufactured goods at 7·4 per cent of the total exports. This figure was

[1] Compiled from *Anuário estatístico do Brasil*, 1949 and 1952, and Ministry of Foreign Affairs, *Brazil, 1940–1*.

Brazil

Table A
Exports from Brazil: Products

	1925 percentage of total exports	1939 percentage of total exports	1946 percentage of total exports	1951 exports in cr. $1,000	Percentage
Coffee	72·0	40·0	35·3	19,447,884	59·8
Cotton	3·2	20·5	17·0	4,463,303	13·7
Cacao	2·6	4·0	3·5	1,298,442	4·0
Vegetable oils & other oleaginous products	0·4	4·4	3·2	1,158,170	3·6
Timber	0·7	2·1	4·8	1,076,484	3·3
Meat, hides, & other pastoral products	3·7	8·3	5·1	890,005	2·7
Minerals	0·3*	0·8*	1·4	579,925	1·8
Fibres	—†	—†	0·2	440,380	1·4
Fruit	0·4	3·1	1·7	437,614	1·3
Vegetable wax	0·5	2·2	3·1	364,329	1·1
Manufactured goods	—†	—†	7·4	310,314	1·0
Tobacco	2·2	1·7	2·7	340,271	1·0
Rice	0·0	0·8	2·1	305,529	0·9
Rubber	4·9	1·9	1·6	52,168	0·2
Remaining exports	9·1	11·1	10·9	1,349,447	4·2
Total	100·0	100·0	100·0	32,514,265	100·0

* Precious and semi-precious stones only.
† Not separately recorded.

The Scene Today: Political, Economic, and Social

TABLE B
IMPORTS TO BRAZIL: MATERIALS OR GOODS

	1925 percentage of total imports	1939 percentage of total imports	1946 percentage of total imports	1951 imports in cr. $1,000	Percentage
Machinery and tools	14·0	19·8	21·3	9,675,944	26·0
Cars and other road vehicles & accessories	12·7	10·5	9·1	5,591,540	14·8
Other iron and steel goods	7·5	8·9	7·0	1,760,672	4·8
Iron and steel	1·3	2·6	3·2	330,328	0·9
Coke, coal, etc.	4·2	4·7	2·8	544,807	1·5
Oil, petrol, and paraffin	4·5	7·1	5·8	3,790,310	10·2
Chemical and pharmaceutical products	2·0	5·8	4·6	2,582,042	4·7
Manufactured goods not included elsewhere	—*	—*	12·2	5,282,658	14·2
Wheat and wheaten flour	8·7†	7·1†	8·0	2,590,095	7·0
Other food products	—*	—*	11·1	2,007,499	5·4
Remaining imports	46·1	33·6	14·9	3,112,450	8·3
TOTAL	100·0	100·0	100·0	37,198,345	100·0

* Accurate figures not obtainable.
† Percentage given for grain wheat only.

Brazil

TABLE C

EXPORTS FROM BRAZIL, BY COUNTRIES

	1925 percentage of exports	1939 percentage of exports	1946 percentage of exports	1951 exports in cr. $1,000	Percentage
U.S.A.	45·3	36·5	42·3	15,935,567	49·0
United Kingdom	5·0	9·6	8·8	3,196,072	9·9
Argentina	5·3	5·5	7·5	2,162,936	6·7
France	12·8	6·3	2·1	1,642,676	5·1
Germany	6·7	12·0	—	1,557,364	4·8
Holland	6·2	3·8	2·9	957,186	2·9
Sweden	2·0	3·1	2·9	869,057	2·7
Belgium	2·6	2·8	4·3	766,180	2·3
Italy	6·3	2·4	4·8	559,940	1·7
Canada	0·1	0·3	0·8	389,884	1·2
Norway	—*	—*	0·8	312,949	1·0
Switzerland	—*	—*	1·3	262,608	0·8
Venezuela	—*	—*	0·8	15,276	—
Dutch W. Indies	—*	—*	0·1	1,685	—
Other countries	7·7	17·7	20·6	3,884,885	12·0
TOTAL	100·0	100·0	100·0	32,514,265	100·0

* Figures not available.

already less than half the inflated 1945 percentage, but it was nevertheless indicative of Brazil's potential possibilities. By 1948 the percentage was down to 3·3 and the 1951 figure of 1·0 reflects the recovery of West European industry. The increase in the coffee percentage is an indication of inflated prices rather than of increased quantities; but in general the position is healthier than ever before, although the dependence on coffee is still too great.

Table B is equally revealing, and reflects a growing preoccupa-

The Scene Today: Political, Economic, and Social

TABLE D

IMPORTS TO BRAZIL, BY COUNTRIES

	1925 percentage of imports	1939 percentage of imports	1946 percentage of imports	1951 imports in cr. $1,000	Percentage
U.S.A.	24·7	33·7	58·3	15,563,462	41·8
United Kingdom	22·1	9·2	8·0	3,158,328	8·5
Argentina	11·7	8·4	7·8	2,313,310	6·5
Germany	13·8	19·2	—	2,073,040	5·6
Dutch W. Indies	—*	3·3	3·8	1,807,224	4·8
France	5·8	2·7	0·9	1,756,590	4·7
Sweden	0·8	2·3	3·0	1,297,485	3·5
Belgium	3·5	4·2	1·4	1,201,289	3·2
Venezuela	—*	—*	0·4	1,078,138	2·9
Italy	3·7	1·8	1·0	819,919	2·2
Holland	—*	—*	0·5	816,497	2·1
Switzerland	—*	—*	2·9	731,499	1·9
Canada	1·4	1·5	2·6	620,650	1·7
Norway	—*	—*	0·5	431,531	1·2
Other countries	12·5	13·7	8·9	3,529,387	9·4
TOTAL	100·0	100·0	100·0	37,198,345	100·0

* Figures not available.

tion with capital goods as well as an increasing capacity for the production of coal, iron, and steel, and also of manufactured consumer goods. Fourteen per cent of all imports devoted to machinery and tools in 1925 becomes 26·0 per cent in 1951. Imports of iron and steel, and other iron and steel goods, rise to 11·5 per cent and 10·2 per cent in 1939 and 1946 respectively, and sink to 5·7 per cent in 1951; coal imports representing 4·7 per cent in 1939 have dropped to 1·5 per cent in 1951. There are no

Brazil

wholly reliable figures for manufactured consumer goods in 1925 and 1939, but the large proportion of Brazil's imports that they represented is reflected in the percentages given for 'remaining imports'. By 1951 manufactured goods not elsewhere included, together with the remaining imports represent a total of 22·5 per cent as against 46·1 per cent, 33·6 per cent, and 27·1 per cent in 1925, 1939, and 1946 respectively. On the other hand, the figure for road vehicles has reached a new peak at 14·8 per cent, a proportion of imports which can no longer be attributable to the need to make good war-time shortages. Important too is the rise in oil and petrol imports, now over 10 per cent, which explains the tenacity with which the search for oil is pursued. Although the percentage of 7·0 is a little lower than that of 1946, the quantity involved is about the same. In 1948, when the percentage was 11·9, the value of wheat imported was a little lower than in 1951.

Table C is the least illuminating. It shows the extent to which Brazil is dependent upon the United States for its export markets, and how increasingly important a position Argentina occupies in Brazil's foreign trade. The exports to France in 1925 (12·8 per cent of the total), to Germany in 1939 (12·0 per cent), and to the United Kingdom in the same year (9·6 per cent) show how important European recovery is to Brazil. By 1951 only Britain, of the main European importers of Brazilian products, had surpassed the 1939 figure.

Finally, Table D shows how during the second quarter of the century the United States dominance of Brazil's foreign trade spread from exports to imports. The inflated figure for 1946 reflects the abnormal situation immediately following the war, but even in 1948 as much as 51·2 per cent of Brazil's imports came from the United States. The 1951 returns show some recovery in European industry, but the relatively high figure for the United Kingdom was not maintained in 1952 and 1953 because of Brazil's payments difficulties. Even in 1951 the United Kingdom's share of trade in Brazil was not comparable to 1925 when it was a good second to the United States (22·1 to 24·7 per cent). Interesting and significant is the relatively high place among Brazil's principal suppliers occupied by the Dutch West Indies and Venezuela, on whose petroleum Brazil is largely dependent.

All these figures should be examined in the light of Brazil's production, which in practically every commodity shows a sub-

The Scene Today: Political, Economic, and Social

SOME PRINCIPAL PRODUCTS OF BRAZIL

Product	Unit	1939	1946	1951
MINERAL				
Coal	tons	1,046,975	1,896,883	1,963,168
Iron-ore	tons	533,282	582,516	2,406,902
Manganese ore	tons	257,752	172,264	203,542
VEGETABLE				
Raw Materials				
Rubber	tons	16,430	31,687	27,677
Carnaúba wax	tons	11,421	11,633	11,312
Cotton	tons	428,523	377,767	348,791
Cotton seed cake	tons	999,882	744,086	619,765
Food & Tobacco				
Maté	tons	93,383	62,582	64,796
Cane sugar	tons	19,987,772	28,068,845	33,652,508
Manioc	tons	7,122,316	12,224,793	11,917,560
Oranges	1,000	6,029,023	5,272,104	6,181,678
Maize	tons	5,393,553	5,721,372	6,218,030
Rice	tons	1,484,514	2,759,026	3,182,080
Beans	tons	789,722	1,075,955	1,237,662
Coffee	tons	1,157,031	917,318	1,080,189
Sweet potatoes	tons	— *	787,888	822,884
Potatoes	tons	503,822	541,743	721,747
Wheat	tons	101,107	212,514	423,646
Cacao	tons	134,759	121,659	121,199
Tobacco	tons	95,998	119,225	117,932
Pastoral				
Beef	tons	802,410†	753,863	954,664
Pork	tons	275,086†	123,395	119,902
Mutton	tons	6,081†	22,265	17,203
Goat's meat	tons	5,128†	11,706	12,801
Hides & skins	tons	46,988†	118,071	147,635
MANUFACTURES				
Consumer Goods				
Tyres & inner tubes	value in cr. $000	89,036‡	606,700	2,172,587
Cotton textiles	1,000 linear metres	893,904	1,142,151	1,119,738§
Heavy Industries				
Pig iron	tons	160,016	370,722	776,248
Steel	tons	90,169	673,744	1,539,528

* Figure not available.
† 1938 figures from Ministry of Foreign Affairs, *Brazil, 1940–1*.   ‡ 1940.
§ 1948 figure; no later figure has been published.

(SOURCE: except where otherwise stated, *Anuário estastístico do Brasil*, 1949 and 1952.)

Brazil

stantial increase between 1939 and 1951 (see table opposite). Perhaps the most striking increase is in coal, iron, and steel. It is undoubtedly true that the Brazilian coal is of inferior quality, and for long it was thought that it would never be possible to mine enough satisfactory coal for coking. In spite of this, production has substantially increased, and there has been a steady fall in imports since 1937. The Second World War, by drastically reducing the amount of coal available for importing, provided a great stimulus to home production, which, by 1945, reached a record figure of over 2 million tons, almost all of which came from the states of Rio Grande do Sul (1,140,075 tons), and Santa Catarina (692,856 tons), with smaller quantities from Paraná (107,208 tons) and São Paulo (18,770 tons). There was a slight fall in 1946 when it again became possible to import foreign coal, but by 1948 it had passed the 2 million mark, and production has remained steady at about that figure.

HYDRO-ELECTRIC POWER

It was seen in Chapter I[1] that the difficulties in the way of obtaining high grade coal, and the small success so far achieved in the search for oil, have made Brazilians conscious of the need for exploiting hydro-electric power. A country as well watered as Brazil should be able to find considerable sources of such power. It is said that Brazil ranks sixth in the list of nations in the matter of potential electric power, with $14\frac{1}{2}$ million h.p. However, it is estimated that the total potential water-power obtainable by storage and diversion may well amount to 60 million h.p.[2] The following table gives an idea of development during recent years:

	Hydro-electric (kw.)	Thermal electric (kw.)	Total (kw.)
1939	884,570	160,153	1,044,723
1951	1,584,756	355,190	1,939,946

These figures show an increase of nearly 90 per cent in twelve years, but there can be no doubt that development in the next few years will be at a much greater rate. Many projects have been

[1] cf. p. 12 above.
[2] Benjamin H. Hunnicutt, *Brazil, World Frontier* (New York, Van Nostrand, 1949).

The Scene Today: Political, Economic, and Social

considered or are being worked out, some with capacities of 1 or 2 million kw. Perhaps one of the most promising is the hydroelectric project to harness the water-power at the Paulo Afonso falls, for which a company was organized in 1947 with a capital of cr. $400 million (over £7 million) of which half was subscribed by the government. Substantial progress on this and other schemes has been made in recent years, and in 1953 the total installed capacity was estimated to be over two and a half million kilowatts.

STEEL

Throughout this study it has become clear that apart from the health and nutrition of the people, and the shortage of transport, Brazil's greatest problems are fuel and power and the consequent lack of heavy industries. The energetic steps being taken to solve the fuel and power problems are matched by the recent development in heavy industry. A total production of steel and pig iron of a quarter of a million tons in 1939 has risen to over 2 million in 1951. Far and away the most important project is that of the National Steel Company built at Volta Redonda, in the state of Rio de Janeiro, in the valley of the river Paraíba, alongside the Central Railway of Brazil, between the capital and the city of São Paulo and about ninety miles from the city of Rio. Steel production began in June 1946, and the plant is already responsible for more than half the country's iron and steel production. The project was financed by a loan of $25 million from the Export-Import Bank of Washington, and a similar sum subscribed in Brazil. All these developments will make a marked difference to the Brazilian standard of living, and increase considerably its potential contribution to the strength of the Western world.

STAPLE FOODS

But as has been seen, the progress of Brazil also depends on its capacity to improve nutrition. The production of staple foods—of rice, beans, manioc, and cane sugar—all show an enormous increase, but examined together with the production of maize, meat, and other foods, such as milk, butter, cheese, potatoes, and other vegetables, this increase is only just enough to cover the huge increase in population, from 41 million in 1940 to between 52 and 53 million in early 1951. Rising standards of living have

Brazil

led to an increased consumption of wheat and wheaten flour, and Brazil is today far from being self-supporting in the matter of wheat. A century ago Brazil was a relatively large wheat-producing country, particularly in the south, in Rio Grande do Sul. An epidemic of rust brought disaster, and lack of transport and the relative cheapness of Argentine wheat discouraged serious efforts at rehabilitation until recently. In recent years, however, the problem has been tackled scientifically and with determination. Both the Federal Government and that of the state of Rio Grande do Sul have done a great deal of experimental work, and a grower can now purchase reliable and selected seed, and obtain the best advice for the care of his crop as well. Wheat production is now some five times what it was in 1939, but in 1951, for example, a production of 423,646 tons compared with imports of wheat and wheaten flour of 1,368,664 tons.

Production in 1951 showed an unexplained fall as compared with 1950 when it amounted to 519,261 tons; but even if later returns show a recovery it is unlikely that the proportion of Brazilian-produced wheat consumed in the country can keep pace with the rapidly rising consumption. The heavy increase in tonnage imported reflects this rise, although it is partly due to increased milling capacity in Brazil (estimated in 1953 as capable of producing over 2 million tons of flour) and to the fact that there is now very little flour imported into Brazil. If it is estimated that the tonnage of flour produced is approximately 75 per cent of the wheat, flour consumption in Brazil has increased from less than 800,000 tons in 1948 to more than 1,200,000 in 1951; even this figure, however, means a consumption per head of less than 24 kg. in the year.

Nevertheless it must be borne in mind that wheat is only now becoming a staple food for the majority of Brazilians. Manioc, maize, rice, and beans are the more traditional foods and the consumption of sugar is strikingly high. The increase in the production of all these, except manioc, has been very substantial. In 1948 the rise in the production of rice so far outstripped the rise in consumption that rice represented $3\frac{1}{2}$ per cent of Brazil's exports for that year. Although exports in 1951 were less than 1 per cent of the total, production increased by nearly 25 per cent between 1948 and 1951. The slight fall in the production of manioc probably reflects a gradual change in Brazilian food preferences, borne out not only by the increase in wheat con-

The Scene Today: Political, Economic, and Social

sumption but also by a slight decline in the production of sweet potatoes since 1948, more than compensated by an increase in potatoes.

COFFEE

Production of coffee in 1948 was about 10 per cent lower than in 1939; in spite of this, the value of the lower production was about four times as great in 1948. The price has continued to rise. This has proved an inducement to coffee growers, in spite of the hardship caused by over-production before the war. Up to 1943 there was still a ban on the planting of new trees, and many of the old trees with a declining yield were cleared to make way for more profitable crops. It is said that there is a relatively small amount of land left which is suitable for the planting of coffee trees, particularly in São Paulo where the heat is not great enough for the crop to require other trees alongside to provide shade. São Paulo has about half the coffee trees of Brazil; it is therefore significant that there has been a substantial decline in the number of trees in that state, in spite of the lifting of the ban on the planting of new trees in 1943. The 1943 total was 1,268,278,462; in 1947 the figure was down to 1,035,322,019. Experiments have been made with the Pará rubber tree to provide suitable shade for the coffee tree with some success. As the Pará rubber tree itself produces latex of good quality, the combination may make possible an expansion of coffee production in warmer areas.

Meanwhile some expansion has been achieved, mainly in the state of Paraná, where new land and younger trees than in the state of São Paulo, have accounted for lower production costs. On the other hand Paraná is perhaps a little more exposed to frosts than São Paulo; certainly Paraná suffered more than São Paulo from the severe frost of July 1953, though this was at least partly due to the much higher proportion of younger trees in the former state. This frost has probably prevented any increase in production that might have been expected from the new planting, and may even lead to some reduction during the next two or three years; the increase has, in any case, been slow and gradual, amounting to about $6\frac{1}{2}$ per cent between 1947 and 1951. The increased price of coffee has led to a renewed over reliance upon it as a source of foreign exchange, of which it is estimated to have earned between 72 and 73 per cent in 1952.

Brazil

Brazilians are, not unnaturally, alarmed at the increased production of coffee in other Latin American countries and in Africa. On the initiative of President Vargas in 1951 and following upon appropriate legislation in 1952, the Instituto Brasileiro do Café was brought into being in 1953. The controlling board of the Institute will include representatives of the growers, exporters, and Federal and State governments; it will supervise the industry, defend prices, promote research, and generally take over the functions and remaining assets of the Departamento Nacional do Café, which was officially closed in 1946, and of the Coffee Economy Division.

COTTON

Cotton is Brazil's second largest export: the war disorganized the cotton trade as by far the greater part was sold in Western Europe. This accounts to some extent for the decline in production since the 1939 figure of over 400,000 tons. Nevertheless, in view of the considerable demands of the Brazilian textile industry, it is surprising to note that the 1951 production was lower than the 1946 (though higher than in 1948 when it was 319,584 tons). British spinners, in particular Mr Arno Pearse, who headed a group of British experts who visited Brazil, have had much to do with the development of cotton in Brazil since 1930. Their advice in the matter of length of staple, ginning, standardization, and grading was heeded by the Brazilian authorities, and the results of their investigations and encouragement made Brazil an important cotton producer; the expanding demand of home industrialists has led to its becoming one of the largest in the world. United States shortages make probable an increase in Brazilian production.

FRUIT AND CACAO

Fruit growing, particularly oranges, suffered a setback during the war when important West European markets were closed or greatly reduced. Nevertheless, consumption has increased, and production is slightly higher than before the war.

Cacao production declined considerably immediately after the war, in spite of encouragement from the state government of Bahia; partly as a result of an admirable marketing organization there has been some improvement and the 1951 figure of 121,199 tons compares favourably with the 1948 production of only

The Scene Today: Political, Economic, and Social

96,910 tons. Brazil is second only to the Gold Coast as a cacao producer, and if the swollen shoot disease in the Gold Coast is not satisfactorily curbed, a further Brazilian expansion in this product may be looked for.

RUBBER

The war, which did so much harm to some aspects of Brazilian economy, not only stimulated the expansion of industry, but also made possible renewed activity in the production of rubber. So far the bulk of Brazil's production has been the result of tapping wild rubber trees, and relatively little progress has been made with plantations on lines similar to those prevailing in Malaya and Indonesia. Nevertheless, the Agronomic Institute of the north, in Belém, capital of Pará, has been carrying out experiments in plantation rubber which may ultimately prove successful. The biggest experiment has been made by the Ford Motor Company, which received a concession in 1927 of 5,000 square miles of territory on the River Tapajós (a tributary of the Amazon) in the state of Pará. The Ford experiment was not a financial success and the concession was relinquished to the Brazilian government for a nominal sum. However, it proved that good health and tolerable living conditions are possible in the Amazon jungle. The development of the Brazilian rubber goods industry (particularly tyres) has provided a steady outlet and, in spite of the development elsewhere of synthetic products, rubber may yet become once again an important element in the Brazilian economy.

OTHER VEGETABLE PRODUCTS

In spite of the inevitable concentration of attention on the principal products and exports, Brazil is now fully conscious of the need to diversify her economy and much attention is paid to such products as Carnaúba wax, jute, and other fibres, vegetable oils, timber, and tobacco.

TERMS OF TRADE

Economists have had much to say about 'terms of trade', and in particular of how they have moved against Western Europe. An exact assessment is difficult in a country with so rapidly expanding an economy as Brazil, but the following table suggests

Brazil

that the terms of trade moved far more heavily against Brazil between 1928 and 1938 than they have done in her favour between 1938 and 1948:

Exports

Year	Quantity in tons	Value in cr. $000	Value per ton in cr. $000
1928	2,075,048	3,970,273	1·9
1938	3,933,870	5,096,890	1·3
1948	4,658,408	21,696,874	4·7
1951	4,851,889	32,514,265	6·7

Imports

Year	Quantity in tons	Value in cr. $000	Value per ton in cr. $000
1928	5,656,977	3,694,990	0·7
1938	4,913,170	5,195,570	1·1
1948	6,803,616	20,984,880	3·1
1951	10,994,491	37,198,345	3·4

(SOURCE: *Anuário estatístico do Brasil*, 1949.)

This can be no more than a rough and ready method of examining terms of trade in view of the changing nature of Brazil's imports. Terms of trade changed against Brazil in 1952; at present the position is favourable to Brazil, though not as much, proportionately, as it has been in the past. Nevertheless, the development of industrial capacity and the reduction of the foreign debt make a favourable balance of payments possible for some time to come, provided controls are not unduly relaxed as in 1951. The budgetary situation is not so favourable, and the temptation to allow deficits is considerable in a country where there is so much to be done; but the need to prevent any further rise in the cost of living may well provide the incentive to economy where this is possible.

BANKING SYSTEM

A glance at Brazil's banking system is necessary to complete this cursory examination of its economy. At the end of 1952 there were over 4,000 banking establishments in Brazil, including 383 credit co-operatives, 314 agencies of the Bank of Brazil, and 42 branches of foreign banks.[1] The total capital of all banks in Brazil amounted to cr. $7,258 million, of which foreign banks accounted for about 7 per cent.[2] Total bank deposits were cr. $128,161 million and bank loans amounted to cr. $123,314

[1] Banco do Brasil, S.A., *Relatório de 1952*, pp. 343-4.
[2] Ministerio da Fazenda, Movimento Bancário do Brasil, 1952 (Rio de Janeiro, 1953).

The Scene Today: Political, Economic, and Social

million;[1] expansion since 1940 has been very great and these figures are probably six or seven times their equivalents twelve years earlier, but the fluctuating value of Brazilian currency makes impossible an accurate comparison. Banking institutions show a profit of about 15 per cent on capital invested, but less than half is distributed to shareholders. Ownership is concentrated in few hands, which accounts for the relatively low dividends and the building up of large reserves. The Bank of Brazil is a mixed corporation of which the state owns a controlling interest (55·73 per cent). The Bank has, in addition to its General Credit Department, and Exchange Department, a Foreign Trade Board, a Rediscount Department, and the Banking Mobilization Fund. The Bank implements the decisions of the Superintendency of Money and Credit, a state monetary council created in 1945 to discharge the functions of a central bank. The Bank is in effect at once a central and a commercial bank. Its commercial departments are financially independent units and, for example, the Rediscount Department lends money to the Bank of Brazil just as it does to a commercial bank.

EDUCATION

Writers on education in Brazil in general maintain that in the Colonial period and during the Empire, no attempt was made to educate the broad masses but only a small nucleus of the ruling classes. This would suggest—as is the case in other Latin American countries—old established universities. In fact Brazil's university education dates from 1920 when in Rio de Janeiro a number of independent faculties were grouped together under a Rectorate which has since become the University of Brazil. Since then, however, progress has been rapid and there are today eleven universities as well as a number of independent institutions of advanced education with a total of some 30,000 students. There has been some concentration on law and medicine, although the recent industrial development has led to larger numbers of students of scientific, engineering, and technological subjects; agriculture is also now an important study. Secondary education has received less official encouragement than primary or advanced. There are probably not quite 1,500 secondary schools in the

[1] Ministerio da Fazenda, Movimento Bancário do Brasil, 1952. (Rio de Janeiro, 1953).

Brazil

country and the number of students is little more than 350,000; about 80 per cent of these schools are privately owned and maintained. In sharp contrast there are well over 50,000 primary schools, and about 4 million children between the ages of seven and eleven are registered as attending them. This figure, however, represents rather less than 80 per cent of the total number of children in the country between those ages.

The ideal educational progress allowed for by the existing system implies four years of primary education followed by seven years of secondary education in the *ginásios* divided into two parts, the first of which lasts four years and allows for no specialization, and the second three years divided into two broad groups known as Classics and Science. There are also secondary schools for more specialized commercial, technical, industrial, and agricultural studies.

But even primary education sometimes falls short of the standards laid down. Although all education in the country is subject to general supervision and to basic principles established by the Federal Government and administered by the National Department of Education and Health, the individual states have a wide degree of autonomy. Manuel Bergstrom Lourenço Filho, in his study on the education of Brazil published in 1950 by the Cultural Division of the Brazilian Ministry of Foreign Affairs, writes: 'In fact, in many states primary education is not only insufficient in quantity but also deficient in quality. Schools are badly installed, they do not always have an adequately trained teaching staff, and inspection and educational guidance are uneven.'

Nevertheless, great strides have been and are being made. The realization of the need for better educational facilities is revealed by the increasing proportion of the national budget devoted to education. In 1932 the figure was 6 per cent whereas in 1950 it amounted to 18 per cent. In addition the fact that 80 per cent of the children of Brazil now receive primary education means that it should be possible greatly to reduce the present proportion of illiteracy, estimated to be rather more than 40 per cent.[1]

PRESS

No study of Brazil could omit a brief review of press and radio. The Brazilian press is small by Western European standards, but

[1] See above p. 20.

The Scene Today: Political, Economic, and Social

it has an importance out of proportion to its circulation; and it makes up for its size by its vigour. The total circulation of the forty principal newspapers in the country is probably about 2 million between morning and evening papers, of which the former have a slightly larger sale. During the first Vargas regime they were completely controlled by the government and lost prestige and interest; since then, they have developed with few exceptions on popular and, in many cases, sensational lines. There are a number of serious papers aiming at a higher standard, as, for example, the *Jornal do Comercio*, a conservative Rio de Janeiro paper with a circulation recently estimated to be 8,000, which supported the Dutra government, and *O Estado de São Paulo*, a liberal and democratic São Paulo paper, with a comparatively high circulation of over 70,000. The most important newspaper group in the country is the Diarios Associados, controlled by Senhor Assis Chateaubriand, the stormy petrel of Brazilian journalism, who can be compared only to Lord Beaverbrook in Britain. In the majority of the papers belonging to this chain are reflected the independent and strongly held views of Senhor Chateaubriand, but there are surprising contradictions and Senhor Chateaubriand has been known to change his views with great rapidity. The chain includes in Rio de Janeiro the morning paper *O Jornal*, with a circulation of about 40,000, and the popular *Diario da Noite*, widely read by the artisan class, with the largest circulation in Brazil (about 100,000) and also papers in São Paulo, Santos, Bahia, Recife, Pôrto Alegre, and other cities; the total circulation is in the neighbourhood of half a million. The most widely read and one of the best presented morning papers in Rio de Janeiro is the independent *Correio da Manha* with a circulation of about 60,000. Another important group which is making progress in São Paulo is that comprising the *Folha da Manha*, *Folha da Tarde*, and *Folha da Noite*. These papers have recently been increasing their circulation, which may now be over a quarter of a million. The three papers are modelled very largely on the lines of the British popular press. An important morning paper in Rio de Janeiro is the *Diario de Noticias* for which a circulation of 100,000 has been claimed, though some believe that the figure is nearer 50,000; like the *Correio da Manha*, the *Diario de Noticias* is independent. Circulation figures reveal interesting reading habits. Over the greater part of the country, morning papers are more widely read than evening papers. In São Paulo the figures are about equal

Brazil

with nearly 400,000 for morning papers and about 350,000 for evening papers. But in Rio de Janeiro there is a sharp contrast. Morning papers have a total circulation of under 300,000, whereas evening papers total over 500,000. All the figures quoted refer to the principal newspapers of the country; there are besides many smaller papers with circulations usually lower than 10,000. The principal papers all have Sunday editions with larger circulations, as a rule, than during the week. Sunday circulations are estimated to total over 2½ million. Only some evening papers are published on Mondays; *O Globo*, for example, with two Monday editions achieves a circulation of 110,000 on Mondays only.

RADIO

The development of radio has led to even greater complications than that of the press. There are in Brazil some 300 radio stations, of which the greater part are small, privately owned, and entirely commercial. The larger newspapers nearly all own stations, and the Diarios Associados own an important group, of which the largest is Radio Tupí of Rio de Janeiro, known as the Emissôras Associadas. Another important group is the Emissôras Unidas. These stations, too, are wholly commercial. The Brazilian radio only takes an interest in politics for a short period before elections. In the majority of cases candidates for political office buy time at ordinary commercial rates and payment is made from the funds of the political parties. The most important station in the country is the state-controlled Radio Nacional; this too, however, is a commercial station, and in the year 1950 earned profits amounting to nearly cr. $6,400,000 (£120,000). In September of 1950 (the last month of the presidential electoral campaign) two hours a day were set aside for political propaganda. Different parties were able to broadcast their views under equal conditions, as to time and cost of time on the air. The parties making use of these facilities were: P.S.D., P.T.B., U.D.N., P.S.P., and P.T.N. The only non-commercial radio station in Brazil is the Radio Ministerio da Educação of Rio de Janeiro, which devotes itself to educational and cultural broadcasts. All radio stations in Brazil are required to broadcast, between 19.30 and 20.00 Rio time, the Hora do Brasil, during which government decrees, official announcements, instructions to shipping and similar broadcasts are made, together with a small

The Scene Today: Political, Economic, and Social

proportion of Brazilian music; before 1945 the Hora do Brasil was an hour in length and included pro-government propaganda. There is a fair amount of listening to foreign broadcasts in Brazil, particularly to Britain and the United States. The B.B.C.'s Brazilian Service has achieved some popularity and commands wide respect; until the drastic reduction in the service to Brazil in 1951 there was a large number of daily rebroadcasts of B.B.C. news bulletins, commentaries, and talks, apart from many occasional programmes. Television has begun in São Paulo and Rio de Janeiro; it is owned by the Emissôras Associadas.

CONSTITUTION

Independent Brazil has had five Constitutions, to four of which reference has been made in earlier chapters. The first was adopted under Dom Pedro I immediately after the independence; the second in 1891, shortly after the establishment of the republic; the third in 1934, nearly four years after the Vargas revolution; the fourth, the so-called 'Estado Novo', in 1937, following the Vargas coup d'état; and the fifth, which still holds good, in 1946, after the elections in which Dutra triumphed. This last Constitution describes the country as the United States of Brazil, 'under the representative system, the Federation, and the Republic'. The Federal Government has the right to maintain foreign relations, engage in war, declare martial law, organize defence, issue money, maintain the postal service, and legislate upon all matters relating to the interest of the people as a whole. Limits are set upon Federal intervention in the states. The states have the right to levy certain taxes and retain a fair proportion of administrative responsibilities. The legislative power, or national Congress, consists of a Senate and Chamber of Deputies, both elected by popular suffrage; Ministers of the Federal cabinet are required to appear before either Senate or Chamber to give information on public affairs or legislation. The executive power is exercised by the president and vice-president, aided by the cabinet ministers. The judicial power consists of the Federal Supreme Court, the Federal Court of Appeals, military tribunals, electoral tribunals, and labour tribunals. The majority of civil and criminal cases are heard before tribunals of the states. Federal and state judges are appointed for life. The Constitution declares that all men are equal before the law; that any citizen may ask and obtain pro-

Brazil

tection against the abuse of authority; that freedom of conscience is guaranteed; that all men and women have the right to vote; and that the ballot shall be secret. Church and State are separated, but religious marriages are recognized when properly registered with the civil authority; there is no divorce. Religious instruction in schools is permitted, but not required. That is the Constitution under which president Getúlio Vargas recently took office in 1951.

CHAPTER VI

THE FUTURE

THE preceding chapters have shown the strength and weakness of Brazil. Its vast size, its rapidly growing population, its immense natural resources, and its favoured position in the world ensure its importance among the nations. The physical barriers to communications, the relatively low standards of living of too many of the people, the over-great dependence on the export of coffee, the insufficiency in some basic foods, and the relatively early stage of development of industry, particularly heavy industry, are outstanding weaknesses. It remains to be seen whether the undoubted intelligence of the people can be seconded by sufficient energy and balanced judgement to ensure a major contribution to Western civilization and advancing material and cultural standards for the growing population. Perhaps the most imaginative and carefully considered plan for achieving this desirable end that has yet been produced was the SALTE plan, to which reference was made in the previous chapter.

Although the plan has now been virtually abandoned, some of the work begun under it is being continued; it was furthermore a reasonably realistic assessment of Brazil's most pressing needs, if not of its capacity. For this reason it is still worth a quick examination. The SALTE plan recognized the main problems of the country. It took its name from the initials of the following words: 'Saúde' (health), 'Alimentação' (nutrition), 'Transporte' (transport), and 'Energía' (power). The plan was drawn up in 1948 and finally approved by Senate and Chamber in May 1950. It envisaged a widespread programme of economic development during the period 1950–4, and an expenditure of 20,000 million cruzeiros (nearly £400 million). This expenditure was to be allocated as follows:

                                                                                      cr. $

Health services, including campaigns against
   malaria, tuberculosis, and other diseases   2,640,056,410
Food production, including research, improvement and distribution of seed of various

Brazil

	cr. $
foods as well as other vegetable products such as cotton, jute, and sisal; and other measures to increase the output and quantity of food produced	2,733,400,000
Transport, including the extension and improvement of railways and roads, the re-equipment of various ports, and aid to be given for airport installations	11,345,620,000
Power, including development of hydro-electric power, electrification, petroleum research, oil-well drilling, and erection of oil refineries	3,190,000,000

The balance was accounted for by reserves and other provisions. Some parts of the plan were put into effect before legislative approval had been obtained. In 1949 cr. $1,300 million, and in 1950 cr. $1,900 million were allocated in anticipation of the relative bill becoming law. The plan was to be financed by means of borrowing internally up to a total of cr. $7,000 million, and the balance by means of annual budgetary allocations, as follows:

		cr. $ million
Borrowing		7,000
Budgetary Allocations:		
	1949	1,300
	1950	1,900
	1951	2,200
	1952	2,400
	1953	2,550
	1954	2,600

Serious financial difficulties soon arose and it became clear that the many critics who had forecast that the plan was too big for the Brazilian economy to stand the strain had been largely justified. There could be no doubt that the continued inflationary pressure and budgetary deficits must, if possible, be brought to an end. To achieve these ends the Minister of Finance, Senhor Horacio Lafer, proposed cuts in annual expenditure of over cr. $2,000 million at the end of February 1951. The biggest cut proposed was in the SALTE Plan, for which the 1951 allocation was to be reduced from cr. $2,200 million to cr. $1,314 million.

Unfortunately, these cuts were not enough. In spite of the

The Future

measures taken by the Minister of Finance, including some restriction of credit, a budget surplus was not achieved until May 1953, and by then the cost-of-living index was calculated to have reached 187 (1946 = 100; cf. table on p. 92). Not only was the internal economic situation alarming, but Brazil had been piling up a huge commercial debt, estimated to have been the equivalent of U.S. $1,000 million in July 1953; of this sum nearly U.S. $500 million was owed to the United States, £62,000,000 to the United Kingdom, and the equivalent of U.S. $100 million each to Holland (including the Dutch West Indies) and Germany. Drastic measures were clearly necessary. In June 1953 an important ministerial reshuffle took place affecting six out of the seven civilian members of the cabinet. Among the most important changes was the replacement of Senhor Horacio Lafer as Minister of Finance by Senhor Oswaldo Aranha. The latter has announced a policy of retrenchment, austerity, and controls, and has already achieved much. Similar policies had been advocated by his predecessor so that perhaps at least as significant were changes in the direction of the Bank of Brazil, not least in the director of its Exchange Department.

In the meantime two factors are generally held to imply the virtual abandonment of the SALTE Plan: first, the closing down at the end of July 1953 of the joint Brazil-U.S. Development Commission set up in December 1950; and second, the fact that in order to meet at least a part of its commercial debt to the United States, Brazil had to accept a credit of U.S. $300 million from the Export-Import Bank. It was already clear that additional loans to finance the Plan (between U.S. $140 and 180 million had already been agreed) were unlikely. Such further loans became still more unlikely when Brazil failed to keep the terms of the agreement under which the credit of U.S. $300 million was conceded; the outstanding commercial debts were not met by 1 July 1953, although it is true that by that date Brazil had only drawn U.S. $120 million of the credit. In the meantime the situation in regard to the United States and the protracted negotiations necessary to arrive at a settlement of Brazil's debt to the United Kingdom, have not improved Brazilian credit, and further loans, for whatever purpose, must be considered unlikely until Brazil puts its economic and financial house in order.

Nevertheless, some progress had been made and some beneficial effects are becoming apparent. Apart from important hydro-

Brazil

electric schemes, some work has been done on railway modernization and road building, and health and education standards are generally improving. In due course a new general plan will have to be worked out, preferably less rigid in conception, to ensure balanced progress. A plan on these lines was prepared under Finance Minister Horacio Lafer. The Lafer Plan is one of economic expansion and re-equipment and embodies many projects first conceived under the SALTE Plan. Like the latter, it is based on obtaining foreign loans for that part of the expenditure which would have to be undertaken in foreign exchange; cruzeiro expenditure is financed in a novel manner: a 15 per cent surtax for five years on everyone paying tax of cr. $10,000 or over per annum, and a 3 per cent tax on the undistributed profits and reserves of companies. The plan gives substantially less attention to health and food than the SALTE Plan and in October 1953 the latest available information was summarized in the following table:

PLAN FOR RE-EQUIPMENT LOANS

	Granted		Under Examination		Projects in Preparation		Total	
	U.S. $ (million)	Cr. $ (million)	U.S. $ (million)	Cr. $ (million)	U.S. $ (million)	Cr. $ (million)	U.S. $ (million)	Cr. $ (million)
Railways	27·8	1,318·5	78	4,680·4	49·6	3,293·3	155·4	9,292·2
Electrical Power	74·1	2,530	56·3	1,830·5	28	570	158·4	4,930·5
Agriculture	23	—	4·1	206	—	—	27·1	206
Industry	1·9	12	—	—	20	—	21·9	12
Roads	3	—	3·7	—	6	—	12·7	—
Ports	—	—	11	730	—	—	11	730
Dredging	—	—	26·8	—	1·5	—	28·3	—
Shipping	—	—	25·3	444·5	—	—	25·3	444·5
Totals	129·8	3,860·5	205·2	7,891·4	105·1	3,863·3	440·1	15,615·2

(SOURCE: *Brazil*, Overseas Economic Surveys, H.M.S.O., 1954, p. 29)

For the time being Brazil is concentrating on completing schemes already begun and on the solution of one of its main problems: lack of fuel. For this latter purpose, a new company has been brought into being, financed by government and private capital, in which a minimum holding of 51 per cent of the common stock ensures government control. The new Petróleo Brasileiro, known as 'Petrobras', was approved by Congress in September 1951, and will take over all further developments in the petroleum industry in Brazil. Foreign firms are allowed to continue to operate any refineries, tankers or distribution organizations they may have already in being, but exploration, exploitation of wells and any expansion of refining or distribution is reserved exclusively to the new company.

The Future

Undoubtedly Petrobras will seek technical services and advice from abroad, but direct participation by foreign firms is expressly forbidden, as is the holding of Petrobras shares by foreign nationals. It has already been recognized that Brazil's resources are not large enough to ensure adequate petroleum exploration or the proper exploitation of what petroleum may be found;[1] it has, therefore, been doubted by many whether the rigidity of the state-controlled monopoly that has been set up can be beneficial to Brazil. There can be little doubt that political considerations are mainly responsible and that economic reality would suggest the encouragement of foreign capital and initiative, particularly in an industry which calls for so high a degree of capital risk and specialist skill and which might go a long way towards solving Brazil's economic problems.

Curiously, the strong political feeling engendered by the problem of petroleum is not reflected in manufacturing industry. In the Overseas Economic Survey of Brazil,[2] Mr Walter Godfrey, Commercial Minister in Rio de Janeiro, writes: '. . . there is in Brazil no hostility to foreign investment in industry, although quite naturally there is less interest in encouraging industries which make no essential contribution to the country's wealth. . . .' While it is true that the remittance of profits, on which there is an additional tax of 15 per cent, was arbitrarily suspended in 1952, and that this and the general shortage of foreign exchange are discouraging, it is nevertheless clear that many manufacturers in Western Europe and the United States can only hope to retain a share of the Brazilian market by establishing local factories, possibly in partnership with Brazilian capital. To quote Mr Godfrey again: 'Brazil's future is bright, and . . . eventually she will be a leading industrial country'.[3] In effect the policy in regard to petroleum must be regarded as the exception rather than the rule.

But petroleum is only one of Brazil's problems. In 1949 it was reported[4] that about one in five children in Brazil die before reaching their first birthday; in spite of that, the population has increased by nearly a third in eleven years. Improved health services will lead to an even higher rate of increase. At the same time available statistics although inconclusive, because they cover too

[1] Joint Brazil-U.S. Technical Commission, *Report*, p. 115.
[2] *Brazil*, Overseas Economic Surveys, H.M.S.O., 1954, p. 41.
[3] op cit., p. 42. [4] Joint Brazil–U.S. Technical Commission, *Report*, p. 130.

Brazil

short a period, indicate a declining productivity of the land under cultivation; in addition, food production tends to take place farther and farther away from the big population centres, thus at once increasing the cost and the strain on Brazil's scanty transport. The expanding population will require a great expansion of industry, as well as of agriculture, if it is to maintain and improve standards of living; and in addition the relatively advanced schemes of social service will require a rapidly increasing productivity if they are to be maintained or expanded. It is clear that an expansion of heavy and consumer-goods industries, an extension of transport facilities, an increase in the area of land under cultivation, conservation and fertilization of the soil, drainage and irrigation, as well as improved methods of farming, must all go in hand with the improvement in health services; and it is fair to assume that improved health will make a powerful contribution to the increased productivity that Brazil so urgently requires. But the future is far from desperate, and Brazilians have more than once given proof of their capacity to overcome serious difficulties. The next twenty-five years may well see Brazil become one of the great Powers of the world, with a population of anything from eighty to a hundred million, more nearly matching its vast area. Brazilian statesmen are faced with a challenge which will require all their energy, imagination, and intelligence to meet.

If they succeed, the influence of Brazil among the nations will be for peace, and her example may yet prove to be an inspiration to the newly independent peoples of the Far East and to the nascent countries of Africa. In recent years writers have variously described Brazil in phases such as 'Land of the Future', 'World Frontier', 'An Expanding Economy'; all these are true of Brazil. But it is perhaps equally true to say, as suggested at the beginning of this study, that it is as a land of experiment, as an example to other nations in the same or lesser stages of development, and as an ex-colonial tropical area on the threshold of complete emancipation, that the real significance of Brazil can best be assessed.

POSTSCRIPT
The Death of Getulio Vargas

This edition was completed before the death of Dr Getulio Vargas. In spite of the popularity that he often enjoyed among the Brazilian people, he was not a typical Brazilian, but akin rather to the *caudillos* of earlier days in Spanish American republics. Small in stature, resolute in character, markedly courageous, and an astute politician, he has left an indelible mark on the Brazilian scene. His suicide on 24 August has been condemned by some Brazilians as flamboyant and unpatriotic; his message to the nation as inflammatory, not least his reference to the 'underground campaign of international groups' and to his political opponents. He may have been recalling the opposition to the setting up of 'Petrobras';[1] but this matter was not the cause of his downfall.

In spite of the efforts of Finance Minister Dr Oswaldo Aranha, inflation has not been curbed: in May the President doubled and in some cases trebled minimum wages, in the face of much opposition and against the advice of his Finance Minister. By the time the increases were applied prices had soared further still and the workers hardly benefited. There were also charges of corruption against the President's *entourage*. In early August an attempt on the life of Carlos Lacerda, editor of the opposition paper *Tribuna da Imprensa*, caused the death of an air force officer. An air force court of inquiry declared that members of the President's bodyguard were implicated, and the Air Force demanded his resignation; finally, the Army forced Vargas to apply for ninety days' leave of absence. Not long after the announcement of this decision came that of the President's death. There can be no doubting the genuine sorrow of many humble folk and the resulting disturbances were far less widespread and violent than might have been expected.

Vice-President João Café Filho, who has constitutionally assumed the presidency, has kept aloof from partisan politics since the last election. He appears to enjoy the confidence of the middle classes and the armed forces and is a far less controversial figure than the late President; if he can gain the support of a sufficient

[1] See p. 116

proportion of the urban population there is no reason why Brazil should depart too far from her tradition of peaceful changes of government. In spite of the dominating position enjoyed by Dr Vargas during nearly three-quarters of a century, his death at the age of seventy-one does nothing to change the fundamental problems and prospects of the Brazilian people.

August 1954 J. A. C.

BIBLIOGRAPHY

Akers, C. E. *A History of South America*. 3rd ed. London, Murray, 1930.
Armitage, John. *History of Brazil*. 2 vols. London, 1836.
Azevedo, Fernando de. *Brazilian Culture; an Introduction to the Study of Culture in Brazil*, tr. by W. R. Crawford. New York, Macmillan, 1950.
Bates, Henry. *The Naturalist on the River Amazon*. 2 vols. London, Murray, 1863.
Brazil, Instituto Brasileiro de Geografia e Estatística. *Anuário estatístico do Brasil*. Rio de Janeiro, annually.
—— *Sinopse estatística do Brasil*. Rio de Janeiro, 1947.
—— Ministry of Foreign Affairs. *Brazil, 1939-40: an Economic, Social and Geographic Survey*. Rio de Janeiro, 1940.
——*Brazil, 1940-1: an Economic, Social and Geographic Survey*. Rio de Janeiro, 1941.
Bryce, James. *South America: Observations and Impressions*. London, Macmillan, 1912.
Carvalho, Delgado de. *Geographia do Brasil*. 8th ed. Rio de Janeiro, Franciso Alves, 1936.
Carvalho, Ronald de. *Pequena história da literatura brasileira*. 6th ed. Rio de Janeiro, Briguiet, 1937.
Denis, Pierre. *Brazil*, tr. by Bernard Miall. London, Fisher Unwin, 1911.
Freyre, Gilberto. *Brazil, an Interpretation*. New York, Knopf, 1945.
—— *The Masters and the Slaves, a Study in the Development of Brazilian Civilization (Casa-grande e senzala)*, tr. and ed. by Samuel Putnam. New York, Knopf, 1946.
Godfrey, Walter. *Brazil*. London, H.M.S.O., 1954. (Overseas Economic Surveys).
Guedalla, Philip, and J. A. Camacho. *The Other Americas*. London, Hutchinson, 1941.
Gunther, John. *Inside Latin America*. London, Hamilton, 1942.
Gusmão, Clovis de. *Rondon*. Rio de Janeiro, José Olympo, 1942.
Hambloch, Ernest. *His Majesty the President*. London, Methuen, 1935.
Herring, Hubert. *America and the Americas*. California, Claremont Colleges, 1944.
—— *Good Neighbours: Argentina, Brazil, Chile, and Seventeen Other Countries*. Yale University Press, 1941.
Hill, Lawrence F., ed. *Brazil*. University of California Press and Cambridge University Press, 1947 (United Nations Series).
Hughlett, Lloyd J. *Industrialization of Latin America*. New York and London, McGraw Hill, 1946.
Humboldt, Alexander von. *Personal Narrative of Travels to the Equinoctial Regions of the New Continent, during the years 1799-1804*, tr. by Helen Maria Williams. 7 vols. London, 1814-29.
Hunnicutt, Benjamin H. *Brazil Looks Forward*. Rio de Janeiro, Instituto Brasileiro de Geografia e Estatística, 1945.
—— *Brazil, World Frontier*. New York, Van Nostrand, 1949.
James, Preston E. *Latin America*. Rev. ed. New York, Odyssey Press, 1950.
Joint Brazil-United States Technical Commission. *Report, with Appendixes*. Washington, U.S.G.P.O., 1949 (U.S.A., Dept. of State pub. 3487).
Kirkpatrick, F. A. *Latin America: a Brief History*. Cambridge University Press, 1938.
Livermore, H. V., ed. *Portugal and Brazil*. London, Oxford University Press, 1953.
Meijer, H. *Rural Brazil at the Cross-Roads*. Wageninger, H. Veerman, 1951.

Bibliography

Mielche, Haakon. *The Amazon*. London, Hodge, 1949.
Mitrany, David. *American Interpretations*. London, Contact Publications, 1946.
Nash, Roy. *Conquest of Brazil*. New York, Harcourt Brace; London, Cape, 1927.
Normano, J. E. *Brazil: a Study of Economic Types*. University of North Carolina Press, 1935.
Prestage, Edgar. *The Portuguese Pioneers*. London, Black, 1933.
Rippy, J. Fred. *Historical Evolution of Hispanic America*. 3rd ed. rev. New York, Crofts, 1945.
Robertson, W. S. *History of the Latin American Nations*. New York, Appleton Century, 1943.
Round Table. 'Brazil Enters the War', December 1942.
Royal Institute of International Affairs. *The Republics of South America: a Political, Economic, and Cultural Survey*. London, Oxford University Press, 1937.
Scully, William. *Brazil, its Provinces and Chief Cities*. London, Murray, 1866.
Simonsen, Roberto. *Brazil's Industrial Evolution*. São Paulo, Escola Livre de Sociología e Política, 1939.
Smith, T. Lynn. *Brazil: People and Institutions*. Baton Rouge, Louisiana State University Press, 1946.
—— and Marchant, Alexander. *Brazil; Portrait of Half a Continent*. New York, Dryden Press, 1951.
Southey, Robert. *History of Brazil*. London, 1810–19.
Trend, J. B. *South America, with Mexico and Central America*. London, Oxford University Press, 1941.
Vianna, Oliviera. *Evolução do povo Brasileiro*. 3rd ed. São Paulo, Companhia Editora Nacional, 1938.
Wagley, Charles, ed. *Race and Class in Rural Brazil*. Paris, Unesco, 1953.
Webster, C. K. *Britain and the Independence of Latin America, 1812–30*. 2 vols. London, Oxford University Press, 1938.
Whitbeck, R. H., F. E. Williams, and W. F. Christians. *Economic Geography of South America*. 3rd ed. New York and London, McGraw Hill, 1940.
Wilkes, Charles. *Narrative of the United States Exploring Expedition during the Years 1838–42*. New York, Putnam, 1856.
Williams, Wilhelmine. *Dom Pedro the Magnanimous; Second Emperor of Brazil*. University of North Carolina Press, 1937.
Wythe, George, Royce A. Wight, and Harold M. Midkiff. *Brazil, an Expanding Economy*. New York, Twentieth Century Fund, 1949.
Zweig, Stefan. *Brazil, Land of the Future*. London, Cassell, 1942.

INDEX

Agriculture, 99, 101–5, 113–14
Air travel, 52–3
Aleijadinho, 57, 60
Alencar, José Martiniano de, 58
Aliança Liberal, 46
Amazon River, 6–7; basin, 7, 10, 16–17, 105
Aranha, Graça, 58
Aranha, Oswaldo, 47, 77, 82
Architecture, 60
Argentina, relations with, 70–1; trade with, 96–8
Army, 44, 83
Ayacucho, battle of, 1, 38

Baixada Fluminense, 84
Banda Oriental, 38, 70–1
Bandeirantes, 32–3, 37, 64, 66
Banking, 106–7
Barbosa, Ruy, 45, 73
Barros, Adhemar de, 87, 89
Bernardes, Artur, 45–6
Braz, Wenceslau, 45
British Broadcasting Corporation, 75, 111

Cabral, Pedro Alvares, 28
Cacao, 30–1, 93, 94, 99, 104
Café Filho, João, 89, 90
Campos Salles, Manoel de, 44, 50
Canning, George, 70
Capitanías, 29
Carvalho, Ronald de, 57
Castro Alves, Antônio de, 58
Catholic Electoral League, 90
Climate, 7–8
Coal, 48, 50–1, 97; imports of, 95, 97, 99
Coffee, 33–4, 43, 49, 93, 94, 99, 103–4
Colonial period, 35–9
Colonization, 63–5
Communism, 47, 80, 85–7
Constitution (1824), 39; (1891), 43; (1934), 80; (1937), 82; (1946), 111
Cost of living, rise in, 92
Costa, Lúcio, 60
Cotton, 31, 33, 93–4, 99, 104
Cruz, Oswaldo, 44, 61
Cunha, Euclydes da, 58

Donatários, 29, 37
Dutra, Eurico Gaspar, 80, 85–6, 91; administration, 91–2

Economic cycles, 29–35; early development, 27–9; present economic position, 93–9
Education, 20, 40, 107–8
Elections (1945), 85–6; (1950), 87–9
Empire, political history of, 39–41; constitution, 39
Engenhos, 30
Exports, 30, 48, 93, 94, 96

Farroupilha revolt, 71
Favelas, 16, 56
Fazendas, 46
Finance, capital investment, 49–51; foreign debt, 54; foreign investment, 53–5, 91–2; note circulation, 92; balance of payments, 106; SALTE plan, 113–15
Fiuza, Yedo, 85
Fonseca, Deodoro da, 41, 43
Fonseca, Hermes da, 44
Food production, 99, 101–2; fruit, 99, 104; meat, 99, 101; rice, 101; see also Cacao; Coffee; Maize; Manioc; Sugar; Vegetable products; Wheat
Ford Motor Company, 105
Foreign relations, 69–78
France, attempts to colonize, 36; trade with, 96, 97, 98
Freyre, Gilberto, 22, 56–7, 59

Gama, José Basilio da, 58
Geography, 5–12
Germany, First World War, 72–3; Second World War, 75–7; trade with, 96–8
Gomes, Carlos, 58–9
Gomes, Eduardo, 80, 85, 87–8
Gonçalves Dias, Antônio, 58

Holland, attempts to colonize, 36
Hoover, President, 75
Hydro-electric power, 12, 49, 100

Immigration, 24, 40, 49, 72
Imports, 93, 95, 97, 98

121

Index

Indians, indigenous tribes, 64; Service for the Protection, 67
Industry, development, 45, 47–53; market for consumer goods, 49; manufactures, 97–8
Integralistas, 47, 80
Iron and steel, imports, 95, 97; production, 99, 101
Iron ore, 10, 48
Isabella, Princess, 41

Jesuits, 31–2
João III (King of Portugal), 29, 37
João VI (King of Portugal), 38, 39, 42, 49, 69, 70

Lafer, Horacio, 116
Lafer Plan, 116
League of Nations, 71
López, Francisco, 3, 40, 71, 72

Macedo, Joaquim Manuel de, 58
Machado, Cristiano, 88
Machado de Assis, 58
Maize, 98, 102
Manioc, 16, 99, 101
Mangabeira, João, 88
Mauá, Viscount of, 49
Maurice of Nassau, Prince, 36
Medicine, 67
Mignone, Francisco, 60
Milhaud, Darius, 59
Minerals, 10–12, 94; see also Iron ore
Miscegenation, 2–3, 22–7, 63; 'bleaching' process, 17-18
Monroe Doctrine, 69, 73
Moraes Barros, Prudente José de, 44
Müller, Lauro, 73
Music, 56, 59

Negroes, 2–3, 18, 23–5, 30, 32
Niemeyer, Oscar, 60

Oil, 11, 116–17
Olinda, Viscount, 71

Painting, 61
Paulista revolt, 47, 79
Peçanha, Nilo, 44–5
Pedro I (Emperor of Brazil), 39–40, 69, 70, 111
Pedro II (Emperor of Brazil), 40–1, 71, 90
Peixoto, Floriano, 43
Penna, Afonso Augusto Moreira, 44
Pessôa, Epitácio da Silva, 45, 46

Pereira de Souza, Washington Luiz, 46, 75
Petróleo Brasileiro (Petrobras), 116–17
Political parties, 85–9
Pombal, Marquis of, 37, 66
Population, composition, 17–19; distribution, 12–14; occupations, 19–20
Portinari, Cândido, 57, 61
Positivism, 61, 90
Press, 108–10
Prestes, Júlio, 46
Prestes, Luis Carlos, 80, 87

Queremistas, 83

Radio, 110–11
Railways, 51
Rainfall, 7
Religions, 90–1
Rio Grande do Sul, revolt of, 40, 71
Rodrígues Alves, F. de Paula, 44
Rondon, Cândido Mariano, 65–8
Roosevelt, Franklin D., 75, 82
Roosevelt, Theodore, 68, 73, 74
Rubber, 34, 93, 94, 99, 105

Salgado, Plínio, 80–1
SALTE plan, 113–15, 116
Santos-Dumont, 61
Scultpure, 57, 60
Slavery, 24, 25, 41, 43
Sugar, 30–1, 99, 101

Tariffs, 43, 50
Timber, 29–30, 93, 94, 105
Tirandetes (Joaquim José da Silva Xavier), 38
Tobacco 30–1, 99, 105
Trade, 30, 33–4, 93–9; coastal, 52; terms of, 106; see also Argentina; France; Germany; United Kingdom; United States
Transport, 51–3

United Kingdom, commercial treaties, 42, 69, 75; financial relations, 54–5, 74; relations with, 69, 70, 71, 75; trade with, 96, 97, 98
United States, 42, 48; financial relations, 54–5; relations with, 73–5; trade with, 96, 97, 98
Uruguay, 3, 39, 70, 71

Vargas, Getúlio Dornelles, 46–7, 75,

122

76, 87–9, 92, 111; first regime, 79–85
Vegetable products, 94, 95, 99, 105; see also Cotton; Food production; Rubber; Timber; Tobacco

Villa-Lobos, Heitor, 59
Wheat, 95, 99, 102
World War, First, 72–3; Second, 75–8